INTRODUCTION

The story of Em. Z. Svitzers Bjergningsentreprise (Svitzer) begins in 1833 when Emil Zeuthen Svitzer, a Danish entrepreneur, established a salvage business after noticing many losses occurring on trade routes to and from Denmark. Its business extended to harbour towage in due course. Over the last two decades, the company has expanded considerably and claims to have 430 vessels working in about 100 different locations throughout the world.

Svitzer partly joined the huge A P Møller Maersk group in 1973, becoming fully owned in 1982. It had entered the UK towage business when it took over the Wijsmuller towage fleet in 2001, only shortly after Wijsmuller had taken over Cory Towage. It should be noted, though, that Svitzer tugs had appeared in the UK in the late 1980s to work on a special contract in the north-east of England (see pages 4/5). Some of the photographs in this book illustrate the time when the vivid blue of the Wijsmuller livery was being changed to Svitzer colours and the Maltese cross design was being added to the funnels. A further takeover in 2007 saw Svitzer assume control of the former Adsteam fleet which had grown out of Alexandra Towing via the Howard Smith group.

Because of the huge size of the Svitzer fleet, we are covering it in two volumes. This first volume looks at the company's tugs working in the UK and it will be followed by the second volume which will cover tugs working outside the UK. We considered several possible ways of organising the photographs. Eventually we settled on a chronological order according to year of construction, the exception being at the end of the book where the latest Milford Haven tugs are grouped together. Except where stated, all tugs constructed after 2002 were built for Svitzer.

Having taken over other fleets, Svit... UK operations. As the years have g... groups of four or more, thus decreas... valiant attempt to name the tugs acco... meaningless once they have been mo...

No guarantee can be given for the accuracy of the data. Different sources provide different figures and we have usually used data provided by *Lloyd's Register*. Modifications are sometimes made by operators and these are not always publicised.

In recent years there have been constant developments in tug design in order to improve power, manoeuvrability and stability while towing, and reference is made in captions as to the propulsion configuration fitted to each tug. Sadly there is insufficient space here to explain the technicalities of Voith-Schneider units, azimuth stern drive (ASD) and tractor tugs. I hope that readers will be encouraged to do their own research on tug propulsion.

Acknowledgements

I wish to thank the many photographers who have made their work available for publication. I also thank my son Dominic for his technical input, and Gil Mayes once again for his proof reading and wise corrections and improvements. Thanks should be recorded to our printers who have once again produced a fine booklet.

Bernard McCall   Portishead   June 2017

Published by Bernard McCall, 400 Nore Road, Portishead, Bristol, BS20 8EZ, England.
Website: www.coastalshipping.co.uk. Telephone/fax: 01275 846178   E-mail: bernard@coastalshipping.co.uk
Printed by Gomer Press, Llandysul Enterprise Park, Llandysul, Ceredigion, Wales, SA44 4JL.   Tel: +44 (0) 1559 362371   Email: sales@gomer.co.uk
ISBN: 978-1-902953-85-4

Front cover : The SVITZER CONSTANCE assists the BAFFIN into Hull on 11 March 2008. For tug details, see page 21. (Simon Smith)
Back cover : The WARRIOR III at speed in the River Clyde. She was completed as HAYAKUNI MARU in 1975 at the Kanagawa shipyard in Kobe. She was renamed MONTENOVO in 1991, CELTIC WARRIOR (1993), WARRIOR III (1996) and CHRISTOS XXV (2013). She is powered by two Niigata 6-cylinder engines with a total output of 2600bhp which are geared to two Z-peller units. She has a bollard pull of 35 tonnes. (Dominic McCall)

Tug: HURRICANE H

Builder: Richard Dunston, Hessle

Engine: 1 x 9-cyl Ruston

Propulsion: 1 x fixed pitch propeller

Bollard pull: 54 tonnes

IMO: 7027382

Year built: 1970

Gross tonnage: 282

Former name(s): MARGAM-97

Later name(s): 07-HURRICANE, 09-VOUKEFALAS

Location: Swansea Bay   Date: 6 September 2005

Comments: Built for Alexandra Towing Co Ltd. Last reported off coast of Somalia in August 2016.

Photographer: Dominic McCall

Tug: POINT GILBERT

Builder: Richard Dunston, Hessle

Engine: 1 x 12-cyl Ruston; 2640bhp

Propulsion: 1 x controllable pitch propeller

Bollard pull: 37 tonnes

IMO: 7210824

Year built: 1972

Gross tonnage: 339

Former name(s):

Later name(s): 07-POINT GILBERT 1, 07-GANGUT, 16-BOZKURT

Location: River Clyde   Date: 23 July 2004

Comments: Built for Cory Towage. Trading widely in Mediterranean and West Africa in 2017.

Photographer: Chris Jones

Tug: MJØLNER

Builder: Hoivolds, Kristiansand

Engine: 1 x 16-cyl Alpha; 2319bhp

Propulsion: 1 x controllable pitch propeller

Bollard pull: 30 tonnes

IMO: 7382342

Year built: 1974

Gross tonnage: 196

Former name(s):

Later name(s): 03-ODIN 1, 04-BOREY

Location: River Tyne   Date: 5 May 1989

Comments: In late 1980s/early 1990s, used to push barges laden with colliery waste for dumping at sea. Possibly still in service as BOREY.

Photographer: Michael Green

Tug: WESWEAR

Year built: 1975

Builder: Haak, Zaandam; rebuilt 1989 at Karstensens Skibsværft, Skagen

Engine: 1 x 10-cyl Alpha; 1450bhp

Propulsion: 1 x controllable pitch propeller

Bollard pull: 17 tonnes

Gross tonnage: 163

IMO: 7533367

Former name(s): BRAGE-89

Later name(s): 94-MIMER, 96-GOLIATH FUR, 01-STEVNS

Location: River Tyne   Date: 5 May 1989

Comments: Unlike MJØLNER, this tug was temporarily transferred to a British subsidiary company.

Photographer: Michael Green

Tug: EMSGARTH

Builder: Werftunion, Emden

Engine: 1 x 6-cyl MWM; 1750bhp

Propulsion: 1 x fixed pitch propeller

Bollard pull: 26 tonnes

IMO: 7424487

Year built: 1975

Gross tonnage: 162

Former name(s): JUIST-84

Later name(s): 04-ILTIZAM

Location: Newport   Date: 14 June 2003

Comments: Built for Ems-Schlepper. Last reported at Laayoune (Morocco) in May 2017.

Photographer: Richard Page

Tug: SHIREEN S
Builder: Richards, Lowestoft
Engine: 1 x 12-cyl Ruston; 2640bhp
Propulsion: 1 x controllable pitch propeller
Bollard pull: 35 tonnes
IMO: 7392684

Year built: 1976

Gross tonnage: 312

Former name(s): KELTY-98
Later name(s): 13-W POWER
Location: Swansea Bay   Date: 1 February 2005
Comments: Built for Grangemouth & Forth Towing Co. Last reported at Damietta (Egypt) in November 2015.
Photographer: Dominic McCall

7

Tug: RYAN

Year built: 1977

Builder: Dorman Long Vanderbijl, Durban, South Africa

Engine: 2 x 16-cyl Blackstone; 4400bhp

Propulsion: 2 x controllable pitch propellers

Bollard pull: 53 tonnes

Gross tonnage: 522

IMO: 7510638

Former name(s): C. M. HOFFE-94

Later name(s): 06-HERCULES

Location: Swansea Bay   Date: 20 July 2005

Comments: Built for The Government of the Republic of South Africa (Railways & Harbours Administration). Last reported in Bahrain in 2011.

Photographer: Chris Jones

Tug: BATTLEAXE

Builder: Hall, Russell, Aberdeen

Engine: 2 x 12-cyl Ruston; 3800bhp

Propulsion: 2 x controllable pitch propellers

Bollard pull: 54 tonnes

IMO: 7636913

Year built: 1978

Gross tonnage: 421

Former name(s): ELSIE-98, LYRIE-96

Later name(s):

Location: Swansea Bay   Date: 2 September 2005

Comments: Built for Shetland Towage Ltd. Reported off the coast of Nigeria in February 2017.

Photographer: Chris Jones

Tug: CARRON

Builder: Scott & Sons, Bowling

Engine: 2 x 6cyl Ruston; 2188bhp

Propulsion: 2 x Voith Schneider units

Bollard pull: 24 tonnes

IMO: 7800069

Year built: 1979

Gross tonnage: 225

Former name(s):

Later name(s):

Location: Greenock   Date: 30 September 2008

Comments: Built for Forth Tugs Ltd. Based at Rosyth and working for UK operator on construction of new Forth road bridge.

Photographer: Dominic McCall

Tug: HALLGARTH   Year built: 1979
Builder: Scott & Sons, Bowling
Engine: 2 x 6-cyl Ruston; 2190bhp
Propulsion: 2 x Voith Schneider units
Bollard pull: 23 tonnes   Gross tonnage: 233
IMO: 7800057
Former name(s):
Later name(s): 08-ST PIRAN
Location: off Portishead
Date: 27 December 2002
Comments: Built for Cory Towage. Now working out of Falmouth

Photographer: Bernard McCall

Tug: HOLMGARTH   Year built: 1979
Builder: Scott & Sons, Bowling
Engine: 2 x 6-cyl Ruston; 2190bhp
Propulsion: 2 x Voith Schneider units
Bollard pull: 23 tonnes   Gross tonnage: 233
IMO: 7800045
Former name(s):
Later name(s): 08-MORGAWR
Location: off Newport
Date: 4 June 2008
Comments: Built for Cory Towage. Now working out of Fowey

Photographer: Dominic McCall

Tug: BARGARTH
Builder: Scott & Sons, Bowling
Engine: 2 x 6cyl Ruston; 2200bhp
Propulsion: 2 x Voith Schneider units
Bollard pull: 24 tonnes
IMO: 7800071

Year built: 1979

Gross tonnage: 225

Former name(s): FORTH-03, LAGGAN-87
Later name(s):
Location: Swansea Bay   Date: 26 April 2006
Comments: Built for Forth Tugs Ltd. Based at Waterford for Irish owner in 2017.
Photographer: Chris Jones

Tug: YARM CROSS

Builder: Richard Dunston, Hessle

Engine: 2 x 6-cyl Ruston; 2640bhp

Propulsion: 2 x directional propellers

Bollard pull: 35 tonnes

IMO: 7800021

Year built: 1979

Gross tonnage: 207

Former name(s):

Later name(s): 12-BSV SCOTIA

Location: River Tyne   Date: 4 March 2006

Comments: Built for Tees Towing Co Ltd. Based at Constanta, Romania, in 2017.

Photographer: Dominic McCall

Tug: FARIS

Year built: 1979

Builder: Dorman Long Vanderbijl, Durban, South Africa

Engine: 2 x 16-cyl Blackstone; 4400bhp

Propulsion: 2 x controllable pitch propellers

Bollard pull: 53 tonnes

Gross tonnage: 522

IMO: 7510640

Former name(s): F. H. BOLTMAN-94

Later name(s): 06-ATLAS

Location: Port Talbot

Date: 20 July 2005

Comments: Built for The Government of the Republic of South Africa (Railways & Harbours Administration). Last reported in Bahrain in 2014.

Photographer: Chris Jones

Tug: AVONGARTH

Builder: Kanagawa, Kobe

Engine: 2 x 6-cyl Niigata; 2600bhp

Propulsion: 2 x Z-peller units

Bollard pull: 32 tonnes

IMO: 8004507

Year built: 1980

Gross tonnage: 241

Former name(s): IWASHIMA MARU-91

Later name(s): 10-PACIFIC CASTOR, 12-LADY JESSE II

Location: River Avon   Date: 8 April 2006

Comments: Built for Naigai Unyu K. K. Last reported off Port Said and in Nigerian ownership in 2016.

Photographer: Dominic McCall

Tug: SEA ENDEAVOUR
Builder: Richards, Great Yarmouth
Engine: 1 x 12-cyl Ruston; 3001bhp
Propulsion: 1 x fixed pitch propeller
Bollard pull: 47 tonnes
IMO: 7915163

Year built: 1980

Gross tonnage: 221

Former name(s):
Later name(s): 06-SEA ENDEAVOUR I
Location: off Portishead   Date: 24 July 2002
Comments: Built for C J KIng & Sons Ltd. Laid up at Nakskov, Denmark,
registered in Panama, and in poor condition in 2017
Photographer: Bernard McCall

Tug: SHANNON

Builder: McTay Marine, Bromborough

Engine: 2 x 8-cyl Niigata; 3200bhp

Propulsion: 2 x Z-peller units

Bollard pull: 42 tonnes

Year built: 1981

Gross tonnage: 382

IMO: 8011835

Former name(s): ELDERGARTH-99

Later name(s): 01-SAFE SUPPORTER I

Location: Royal Portbury Dock, Bristol   Date: 26 September 2008

Comments: Built for Cory Towage. The first British-built ASD tug.

Converted to a research vessel in 2009 and then back to a tug in 2015.

Photographer: Dominic McCall

Tug: ROWANGARTH

Builder: McTay Marine, Bromborough

Engine: 2 x 8-cyl Niigata; 3200bhp

Propulsion: 2 x Z-peller units

Bollard pull: 42 tonnes

IMO: 8011847

Year built: 1981

Gross tonnage: 382

Former name(s):

Later name(s):

Location: River Tyne   Date: 20 January 2006

Comments: Built for Cory Towage. Retains same name for owners in Nikolaev, Ukraine, in 2017.

Photographer: Dominic McCall

Tug: SVITZER ELIZABETH

Builder: Cochrane, Selby

Engine: 2 x 6-cyl Ruston; 2640bhp

Propulsion: 2 x Voith Schneider units

Bollard pull: 32 tonnes

IMO: 8003644

Year built: 1981

Gross tonnage: 268

Former name(s): HT SABRE-06, ADSTEAM ELIZABETH-05

Later name(s): 09-ROOKE

Location: Hull   Date: 29 October 2008

Comments: Built for Humber Tugs Ltd. Based at Gibraltar in 2017.

Photographer: Kevin Jones

Tug: COATHAM CROSS
Builder: Richard Dunston, Hessle
Engine: 2 x 6-cyl Ruston; 2640bhp
Propulsion: 2 x directional propellers
Bollard pull: 35 tonnes
IMO: 7928043

Year built: 1981

Gross tonnage: 207

Former name(s):
Later name(s): 11-CORMILAN, 14-LA DANI
Location: River Tyne   Date: 21 June 2007
Comments: Built for Tees Towing Co Ltd. Sold to Fowey in 2011;
damaged in 2014; sold to Dominica & working out of Philipsburg in 2017.
Photographer: Dominic McCall

Tug: SVITZER CONSTANCE
Builder: Cochrane, Selby
Engine: 2 x 6-cyl Ruston; 2640bhp
Propulsion: 2 x Voith Schneider units
Bollard pull: 32 tonnes
IMO: 8102141

Year built: 1982

Gross tonnage: 268

Former name(s): LADY CONSTANCE-07
Later name(s): 14-CANNIS
Location: River Humber   Date: 5 July 2008
Comments: Built for Humber Tugs Ltd. Based at Fowey in 2017.

Photographer: Bernard McCall

Tug: VØLUND

Builder: Aarhus Flydedok

Engine: 1 x 8-cyl Wärtsilä; 3712bhp

Propulsion: 1 controllable pitch propeller

Bollard pull: 55 tonnes

IMO: 8131116

Year built: 1983

Gross tonnage: 291

Former name(s):

Later name(s): 06-TROENSE II, 09-VT PROTON

Location: River Tees   Date: 19 October 1993

Comments: Still owned in Denmark in 2017 but often trading out of Riga.

Photographer: Michael Green

Tug: SVITZER MORAG   Year built: 1983   Former name(s): LADY MORAG-08, KESTREL-91, KUROSHIO-91

Builder: Hanasaki, Yokosuka   Later name(s): 16-LEON

Engine: 2 x 6-cyl Niigata; 3400bhp   Location: River Medway   Date: 9 July 2011

Propulsion: 2 x Z-peller units   Comments: Built for Daito Unyu K.K. Working out of Piraeus in 2017

Bollard pull: 45 tonnes   Gross tonnage: 365

IMO: 8312007   Photographer: the late Martin Wright

Tug: HT CUTLASS

Builder: McTay Marine, Bromborough

Engine: 2 x 6-cyl Ruston; 2672bhp

Propulsion: 2 x Voith Schneider units

Bollard pull: 32 tonnes

IMO: 8316039

Year built: 1984

Gross tonnage: 287

Former name(s): COBHAM-07, DEXTROUS-00

Later name(s):

Location: off Portishead   Date: 28 May 2012

Comments: Built for Dover Harbour Board. Working out of Puerto Cabello, Venezuela, in 2017, still named HT CUTLASS.

Photographer: Bernard McCall

Tug: OAKGARTH
Builder: McTay Marine, Bromborough
Engine: 2 x 6-cyl Ruston; 4000bhp
Propulsion: 2 x Z-peller units
Bollard pull: 50 tonnes
IMO: 8407711

Year built: 1984

Gross tonnage: 452

Former name(s):
Later name(s): 13-MENTOR
Location: River Mersey   Date: 23 July 2008
Comments: Built for Cory Towage. Working in Sweden and the Baltic in 2017.
Photographer: Dominic McCall

Tug: LADY SUSAN   Year built: 1984   Former name(s):
Builder: Argibay, Alverca, Spain   Later name(s): 09-SVITZER SUSAN
Engine: 2 x 6-cyl Ruston; 2640bhp   Location: River Humber   Date: 5 July 2008
Propulsion: 2 x Voith Schneider units   Comments: Built for Humber Tugs Ltd.
Bollard pull: 32 tonnes   Gross tonnage: 285

IMO: 8224511   Photographer: Bernard McCall

Tug: LADY STEPHANIE

Builder: Argibay, Alverca, Spain

Engine: 2 x 6-cyl Ruston; 2640bhp

Propulsion: 2 x Voith Schneider units

Bollard pull: 32 tonnes

IMO: 8224523

Year built: 1984

Gross tonnage: 285

Former name(s):

Later name(s): 09-SVITZER STEPHANIE, 10-ACHILLES,
            12-FFS ACHILLES

Location: Immingham   Date: 13 May 2008

Comments: Built for Humber Tugs Ltd.

3/3/17-sank off Farsund; 4/17-arrived Fredrikshavn for recycling by Jatop.

Photographer: Simon Smith

Tug: SIR BEVOIS

Builder: McTay Marine, Bromborough

Engine: 2 x 6-cyl Kromhout; 2720bhp

Propulsion: 2 x directional propellers

Bollard pull: 34 tonnes

IMO: 8414166

Year built: 1985

Gross tonnage: 250

Former name(s):

Later name(s): 07-SVITZER BEVOIS, 14-TUG BEAVER

Location: Southampton   Date: 2 June 2007

Comments: Built for Red Funnel Towage Ltd. Working at Gävle, Sweden, in 2017.

Photographer: Bernard McCall

Tug: STACKGARTH

Builder: Richard Dunston, Hessle

Engine: 2 x 6-cyl Ruston; 3400bhp

Propulsion: 2 x directional propellers

Bollard pull: 43 tonnes

IMO: 8410225

Year built: 1985

Gross tonnage: 216

Former name(s): ESTON CROSS-94

Later name(s): 10-FASTNET NORE

Location: off Portishead   Date: August 2002

Comments: Built for Tees Towing Co Ltd. Based in Waterford in 2017.

Photographer: Bernard McCall

Tug: DALEGARTH
Builder: Hanasaki, Yokosuka
Engine: 2 x 6-cyl Niigata; 3200bhp
Propulsion: 2 x Z-peller units
Bollard pull: 45 tonnes
IMO: 8420933

Year built: 1985

Gross tonnage: 360

Former name(s): STRONGBOW-92, KESTREL-90,
launched as YOKOSUKA MARU No. 1
Later name(s): 16-LRS EUROPA
Location: Milford Haven   Date: 24 August 2004
Comments: Built for builder's account. Working out of Constanta in 2017.
Photographer: Chris Jones

Tug: SVITZER ANGLIA

Builder: McTay Marine, Bromborough

Engine: 2 x 6-cyl Ruston; 3492bhp

Propulsion: 2 x Voith Schneider units

Bollard pull: 38 tonnes

IMO: 8415146

Year built: 1985

Gross tonnage: 339

Former name(s): ADSTEAM ANGLIA-08, SUN ANGLIA-06

Later name(s):

Location: River Thames   Date: 31 October 2008

Comments: Built for Alexandra Towing Co Ltd. Still named SVITZER ANGLIA and working in Venezuela & Puerto Rico in 2017.

Photographer: Laurie Rufus

Tug: FLYING SPINDRIFT
Builder: Richard Dunston, Hessle
Engine: 2 x 6-cyl Ruston; 3100bhp
Propulsion: 2 x directional propellers
Bollard pull: 39 tonnes
IMO: 8500953

Year built: 1986

Gross tonnage: 259

Former name(s):
Later name(s): 12-FFS ATLAS
Location: River Tyne   Date: 19 September 2004
Comments: Built for Clyde Shipping Co. Owned in Norway and working in Scandinavia in 2017.
Photographer: Dominic McCall

Tug: YEWGARTH
Builder: McTay Marine, Bromborough
Engine: 2 x 6-cyl Ruston; 3446bhp
Propulsion: 2 x directional propellers
Bollard pull: 50 tonnes
IMO: 8407723

Year built: 1985

Gross tonnage: 452

Former name(s):
Later name(s): 12-BSV IRLANDA
Location: Swansea Bay   Date: 6 September 2005
Comments: Built for Cory Towage. Based in Constanta, Romania, in 2017.
Photographer: Dominic McCall

Tug: SVITZER KEELBY Year built: 1986
Builder: Carrington Slipways Pty Ltd, Tomago, Australia
Engine: 2 x 8-cyl Yanmar; 4802bhp
Propulsion: 2 x Duck Z-peller units
Bollard pull: 65 tonnes Gross tonnage: 470
IMO: 8501397

Former name(s): ADSTEAM KEELBY-07, REDCLIFFE-05, W J TROTTER-01
Later name(s): 15-KEELBY
Location: Immingham Date: 7 December 2008
Comments: Built for Queensland Tug & Salvage Co Pty Ltd. Working in Odessa for Ukrainian owners in 2017.
Photographer: Simon Smith

Tug: WILLOWGARTH

Builder: Richards, Lowestoft

Engine: 2 x 6-cyl Ruston; 3448bhp

Propulsion: 2 x directional propellers

Bollard pull: 45 tonnes

IMO: 8811546

Year built: 1989

Gross tonnage: 382

Former name(s):

Later name(s):

Location: Royal Portbury lock   Date: 13 May 2006

Comments: Built for Cory Towage.

Photographer: Richard Page

Tug: ROSEBERRY CROSS
Builder: Richard Dunston, Hessle
Engine: 2 x 6-cyl Ruston; 3400bhp
Propulsion: 2 x Voith Schneider units
Bollard pull: 37 tonnes
IMO: 8812590

Year built: 1989

Gross tonnage: 290

Former name(s):
Later name(s):
Location: River Tyne
Comments: Built for Tees Towing Co Ltd.

Date: 19 September 2004

Photographer: Dominic McCall

Tug: SVITZER LACEBY

Builder: McTay Marine, Bromborough

Engine: 2 x 6-cyl Ruston; 4732bhp

Propulsion: 2 x Voith Schneider units

Bollard pull: 53 tonnes

IMO: 8919178

Year built: 1990

Gross tonnage: 364

Former name(s): ADSTEAM LACEBY-07, LADY ANYA-05

Later name(s):

Location: River Thames   Date: 14 November 2008

Comments: Built for Howard Smith Towage Ltd.

Photographer: Laurie Rufus

Tug: SVITZER MERCIA

Builder: McTay Marine, Bromborough

Engine: 2 x 6-cyl Ruston; 3862bhp

Propulsion: 2 x Voith Schneider units

Bollard pull: 44 tonnes

IMO: 8914685

Year built: 1990

Gross tonnage: 449

Former name(s): ADSTEAM MERCIA-08, SUN MERCIA-05

Later name(s):

Location: River Thames   Date: 14 November 2008

Comments: Built for Alexandra Towing Co Ltd.

Photographer: Laurie Rufus

Tug: HT BLADE

Builder: Richards, Great Yarmouth

Engine: 2 x 6-cyl Ruston; 3514bhp

Propulsion: 2 x directional propellers

Bollard pull: 43 tonnes

IMO: 8902266

Year built: 1990

Gross tonnage: 371

Former name(s): ADSTEAM DEBEN-07, DEBEN-05

Later name(s): 12-STS STAR

Location: River Thames   Date: 14 November 2008

Comments: Built for Alexandra Towing Co Ltd. Owned in Russia and usually working in Kerch Strait in 2017.

Photographer: Laurie Rufus

Tug: SVITZER CECILIA

Builder: McTay Marine, Bromborough

Engine: 2 x 6-cyl Ruston; 4732bhp

Propulsion: 2 x Voith Schneider units

Bollard pull: 53 tonnes

IMO: 8919207

Year built: 1991

Gross tonnage: 364

Former name(s): LADY CECILIA-09

Later name(s):

Location: Lowestoft

Comments: Built for Humber Tugs Ltd.

Photographer: Ashley Hunn

Date: 20 September 2009

Tug: GRAY-VIXEN

Builder: Deltawerf, Sliedrecht

Engine: 2 x 6-cyl Cummins; 900bhp

Propulsion: 2 x fixed pitch propellers

Bollard pull: 13 tonnes

IMO: -

Year built: 1991

Gross tonnage: 40

Former name(s):

Later name(s):

Location: Felixstowe   Date: 15 June 2012

Comments: Owned by Felixarc Marine Ltd. In this image, about to sail to sea to dispose of ashes of deceased person.

Photographer: Bernard McCall

Tug: SVITZER TRIMLEY

Builder: Richards, Great Yarmouth

Engine: 2 x 6-cyl Ruston; 3514bhp

Propulsion: 2 x directional propellers

Bollard pull: 50 tonnes

IMO: 9001693

Year built: 1991

Gross tonnage: 371

Former name(s): ADSTEAM TRIMLEY-07, TRIMLEY-06,

Later name(s): 13-SVITZER TRAVE, 14 SVITZER TRIMLEY

Location: Lowestoft   Date: 9 November 2009

Comments: Built for Alexandra Towing Co Ltd. Svitzer logo here removed from funnel and tug believed to be on hire to Felixarc Marine Ltd, a subsidiary company.

Photographer: Ashley Hunn

Tug: SVITZER SUSSEX
Builder: Richards, Great Yarmouth
Engine: 2 x 6-cyl Ruston; 3826bhp
Propulsion: 2 x Voith Schneider units
Bollard pull: 42 tonnes
IMO: 9019470

Year built: 1991

Gross tonnage: 378

Former name(s): ADSTEAM SUSSEX-07, SUN SUSSEX-05
Later name(s):
Location: Southampton Water   Date: 24 September 2007
Comments: Built for Alexandra Towing Co Ltd.

Photographer: Phil Kempsey

Tug: ADSTEAM SURREY
Builder: Richards, Great Yarmouth
Engine: 2 x 6-cyl Ruston; 3826bhp
Propulsion: 2 x Voith Schneider units
Bollard pull: 42 tonnes
IMO: 9019468

Year built: 1991

Gross tonnage: 378

Former name(s): SUN SURREY-05
Later name(s): 10-SVITZER SURREY
Location: Southampton   Date: 16 July 2007
Comments: Built for Alexandra Towing Co Ltd.

Photographer: Phil Kempsey

Tug: SVITZER SARAH
Builder: McTay Marine, Bromborough
Engine: 2 x 6-cyl Ruston; 4732bhp
Propulsion: 2 x Voith Schneider units
Bollard pull: 53 tonnes
IMO: 8919192

Year built: 1991

Gross tonnage: 364

Former name(s): ADSTEAM SARAH-07, LADY SARAH-06
Later name(s):
Location: Southampton   Date: 16 July 2007
Comments: Built for Howard Smith Towage Ltd.

Photographer: Phil Kempsey

Tug: FIERY CROSS
Builder: Richard Dunston, Hessle
Engine: 2 x 6-cyl Ruston; 3946bhp
Propulsion: 2 x Voith Schneider units
Bollard pull: 41 tonnes
IMO: 9064712

Year built: 1993

Gross tonnage: 296

Former name(s):
Later name(s):
Location: Tees Bay
Comments: Built for Cory Towage.

Photographer: Dominic McCall

Date: 28 January 2006

Tug: PHOENIX CROSS
Builder: Richard Dunston, Hessle
Engine: 2 x 6-cyl Ruston; 3946bhp
Propulsion: 2 x Voith Schneider units
Bollard pull: 41 tonnes
IMO: 9064724

Year built: 1993

Gross tonnage: 296

Former name(s):
Later name(s):
Location: Tees Bay   Date: 11 December 2006
Comments: Built for Cory Towage.

Photographer: Dominic McCall

47

Tug: ALICE K

Builder: Gorokhovetskiy, Russia

Engine: 2 x 8-cyl Pervomaysk; 1598bhp

Propulsion: 2 x controllable pitch propellers

Bollard pull: 25 tonnes

IMO: 8881618

Year built: 1994

Gross tonnage: 182

Former name(s):

Later name(s): 05-GANDVIK

Location: Sharpness   Date: 16 March 2003

Comments: Built for Russian owners but delivered to West Coast Towing Co Ltd. Owned in Russia and working in Kerch Strait in 2017.

Photographer: Bernard McCall

Tug: SVITZER REDBRIDGE
Builder: Yorkshire Dry Dock, Hull
Engine: 2 x 9-cyl Kromhout; 4106bhp
Propulsion: 2 x Voith Schneider units
Bollard pull: 45 tonnes
IMO: 9116888

Year built: 1995

Gross tonnage: 399

Former name(s): ADSTEAM REDBRIDGE-08, REDBRIDGE-05
Later name(s):
Location: River Thames   Date: 22 August 2009
Comments: Built for Red Funnel Towage Ltd.

Photographer: Ashley Hunn

Tug: PORTGARTH

Builder: Hull - Sevmash; completion - Damen, Gorinchem

Engine: 2 x 9-cyl Kromhout; 4052bhp

Propulsion: 2 x directional propellers

Bollard pull: 50 tonnes

IMO: 9067685

Year built: 1995

Gross tonnage: 262

Former name(s):

Later name(s):

Location: Bristol Channel

Comments: Built for Cory Towage.

Date: 3 October 2006

Photographer: Dominic McCall

Tug: LADY MADELEINE   Year built: 1996
Builder: Hull - Polnonca, Gdansk; completed - Damen, Gorinchem
Engine: 2 x 6-cyl Ruston; 4894bhp
Propulsion: 2 x Z-peller units
Bollard pull: 63 tonnes   Gross tonnage: 381
IMO: 9127368

Former name(s):
Later name(s): 08-SVITZER MADELEINE
Location: Solent   Date: 29 May 2007
Comments: Built for Howard Smith Towage Ltd.

Photographer: Phil Kempsey

Tug: SVITZER LYNDHURST

Builder: McTay Marine, Bromborough

Engine: 2 x 6-cylinder Ruston; 4016bhp

Propulsion: 2 x Voith Schneider units

Bollard pull: 43 tonnes

IMO: 9129495

Year built: 1996

Gross tonnage: 379

Former name(s): ADSTEAM LYNDHURST-09, LYNDHURST-06

Later name(s):

Location: Port Talbot

Date: 5 February 2010

Comments: Built for Howard Smith Towage Ltd.

Photographer: Danny Lynch

Tug: ANGLEGARTH

Builder: Hull - Polnonca, Gdansk; completed - Damen, Gorinchem

Engine: 2 x 6-cyl Stork-Wärtsilä; 5166bhp

Propulsion: 2 x Z-peller units

Bollard pull: 66 tonnes

IMO: 9144110

Year built: 1996

Gross tonnage: 374

Former name(s):

Later name(s):

Location: Milford Haven

Comments: Built for Cory Towage.

Date: 12 April 2009

Photographer: Dominic McCall

Tug: SVITZER BENTLEY

Year built: 1996

Builder: Hull - Polnonca, Gdansk; completed - Damen, Gorinchem

Engine: 2 x 6-cyl Ruston; 4898bhp

Propulsion: 2 x Z-peller units

Bollard pull: 60 tonnes

Gross tonnage: 381

54 IMO: 9127356

Former name(s): BENTLEY-09

Later name(s):

Location: Southampton   Date: 16 April 2011

Comments: Built for Howard Smith Towage Ltd.

Photographer: Alan Faulkner

Tug: SVITZER ALMA

Builder: McTay Marine, Bromborough

Engine: 2 x 6-cyl Ruston; 5526bhp

Propulsion: 2 x Voith Schneider units

Bollard pull: 60 tonnes

IMO: 9141144

Year built: 1996

Gross tonnage: 369

Former name(s): LADY ALMA-07

Later name(s):

Location: Immingham   Date: 13 September 2008

Comments: Built for Howard Smith Towage Ltd.

Photographer: Simon Smith

Tug: MILLGARTH
Year built: 1997
Builder: Hull - Polnonca, Gdansk; completed - Damen, Gorinchem
Engine: 2 x 6-cyl Stork-Wärtsilä; 5166bhp
Propulsion: 2 x Z-peller units
Bollard pull: 66 tonnes
Gross tonnage: 374
IMO: 9144122

Former name(s):
Later name(s):
Location: Milford Haven
Date: 14 June 2009
Comments: Built for Cory Towage.

Photographer: Steve Kerrison

: SVITZER ELLERBY   Year built: 1998
der: Imamura, Kobe
ine: 2 x 6-cyl Niigata; 3602bhp
pulsion: 2 x Z-peller units
ard pull: 50 tonnes
ss tonnage: 267
D: 9185231
mer name(s) ADSTEAM ELLERBY-07, LADY EMMA H-05
        LADY EMMA-98, CHEK CHAU-98
er name(s):
ation: off Portishead   Date: 18 August 2013
mments: Built for Hong Kong Salvage and Towage Co Ltd.

otographer: Bernard McCall

: SVITZER MOIRA   Year built: 1998
lder: Imamura, Kobe
gine: 2 x 6-cyl Niigata; 3602bhp
pulsion: 2 x Z-peller units
lard pull: 50 tonnes
ss tonnage: 267
D: 9185229
mer name(s): LADY MOIRA-07, PENG-99
        PENG CHAU-99
er name(s):
ation: off Portishead   Date: 15 June 2013
mments: Built for Hong Kong Salvage and Towage Co Ltd.

otographer: Bernard McCall

Tug: ORMESBY CROSS
Builder: Zamakona, Santurce, Bilbao
Engine: 2 x 6-cyl Niigata; 4400bhp
Propulsion: 2 x Z-peller units
Bollard pull: 60 tonnes
IMO: 9206944

Year built: 2000

Gross tonnage: 433

Former name(s):
Later name(s):
Location: Tees Bay   Date: 28 January 2006
Comments: Built for Cory Towage but delivered to Wijsmuller.

Photographer: Dominic McCall

Tug: AYTON CROSS
Builder: Zamakona, Santurce, Bilbao
Engine: 2 x 6-cyl Niigata; 4400bhp
Propulsion: 2 x Z-peller units
Bollard pull: 60 tonnes
IMO: 9206956

Year built: 2000

Gross tonnage: 433

Former name(s):
Later name(s):
Location: Milford Dock   Date: 20 December 2007
Comments: Built for Cory Towage but delivered to Wijsmuller.

Photographer: Bernard McCall

Tug: SVITZER VICTORY   Year built: 2000

Builder: Hull - Oceanfast Marine Pty Ltd, Fremantle. Completed - Northport Engineering Ltd, Whangarei, New Zealand.

Engine: 2 x 6-cyl Daihatsu; 4968bhp

Propulsion: 2 x Z-peller units

Bollard pull: 73 tonnes   Gross tonnage: 495

IMO: 9193020

Former name(s): ADSTEAM VICTORY-07, GURRONG-05

Later name(s):

Location: River Thames   Date: 26 September 2008

Comments: Built for Howard Smith Towage Ltd.

Photographer: Laurie Rufus

Tug: SVITZER BRUNEL
Builder: Zamakona, Santurce, Bilbao
Engine: 2 x 6-cyl Niigata; 4400bhp
Propulsion: 2 x Z-peller units
Bollard pull: 59 tonnes
IMO: 9273753

Year built: 2003

Gross tonnage: 366

Former name(s): Launched as SEVERNGARTH
Later name(s):
Location: Royal Portbury lock   Date: 3 June 2008
Comments:

Photographer: Kevin Jones

Tug: SVITZER BOOTLE

Builder: Zamakona, Santurce, Bilbao

Engine: 2 x 6-cyl Niigata; 4400bhp

Propulsion: 2 x Z-peller units

Bollard pull: 59 tonnes

IMO: 9286683

Year built: 2003

Gross tonnage: 366

Former name(s):

Later name(s):

Location: Tees Bay

Comments:

Date: 11 December 2006

Photographer: Dominic McCall

Tug: SVITZER BIDSTON
Builder: Zamakona, Santurce, Bilbao
Engine: 2 x 6-cyl Niigata; 4400bhp
Propulsion: 2 x Z-peller units
Bollard pull: 59 tonnes
IMO: 9286695

Year built: 2004

Gross tonnage: 366

Former name(s):
Later name(s):
Location: Eastham
Comments:

Date: 24 September 2006

Photographer: Alan Faulkner

Tug: SVITZER MILFORD

Builder: Baltijos, Klaipeda

Engine: 2 x 6-cyl MaK; 4894bhp

Propulsion: 2 x Z-peller units

Bollard pull: 60 tonnes

IMO: 9292864

Year built: 2004

Gross tonnage: 384

Former name(s): Launched as SVITZER MJØLNER

Later name(s):

Location: Greenock   Date: 13 July 2011

Comments:

Photographer: Bernard McCall

Tug: SVITZER INTREPID
Builder: Kanagawa, Kobe
Engine: 2 x 6-cyl Niigata; 4998bhp
Propulsion: 2 x Z-peller units
Bollard pull: 65 tonnes
IMO: 9342334

Year built: 2005

Gross tonnage: 395

Former name(s): ADSTEAM INTREPID-07, CHAMPION-07,
          TADAMI MARU-07
Later name(s):
Location: off Felixstowe   Date: 13 August 2013
Comments: Built for Soma Harbour Towage Co Ltd.
Photographer: Barry Crickmore

Tug: SVITZER MALLAIG

Builder: Baltijos, Klaipeda

Engine: 2 x 16-cyl Caterpillar; 5710bhp

Propulsion: 2 x directional propellers

Bollard pull: 73 tonnes

IMO: 9317901

Year built: 2005

Gross tonnage: 385

Former name(s):

Later name(s):

Location: River Clyde   Date: 25 July 2008

Comments: Established Svitzer presence at Bremerhaven in late
December 2013.

Photographer: Dominic McCall

Tug: SVITZER MALTBY

Builder: Baltijos, Klaipeda

Engine: 2 x 16-cyl Caterpillar; 5710bhp

Propulsion: 2 x directional propellers

Bollard pull: 73 tonnes

IMO: 9324784

Year built: 2005

Gross tonnage: 385

Former name(s):

Later name(s):

Location: Blyth

Comments:

Date: 6 October 2007

Photographer: Dominic McCall

Tug: SVITZER STANFORD   Year built: 2005
Builder: Hull - Damen, Gdynia; completed - Damen, Gorinchem
Engine: 2 x 6-cyl MaK; 5384bhp
Propulsion: 2 x directional propellers
Bollard pull: 66 tonnes   Gross tonnage: 374
IMO: 9316402

Former name(s): STANFORD-12
Later name(s):
Location: Harwich Haven   Date: 21 February 2014
Comments: Built for Targe Towing Ltd and contracted to provide towage services at BP's Coryton oil terminal on the River Thames.
Photographer: Derek Sands

Tug: SVITZER HARTY   Year built: 2006   Former name(s): ADSTEAM HARTY-07
Builder: Hull - Song Cam, Haiphong; completed - Damen, Gorinchem   Later name(s):
Engine: 2 x 16-cyl Caterpillar; 5710bhp   Location: Sheerness   Date: 20 June 2008
Propulsion: 2 x Z-peller units   Comments: Built for Adsteam.
Bollard pull: 68 tonnes   Gross tonnage: 207
IMO: 9366861   Photographer: Dominic McCall

Tug: ADSTEAM WARDEN   Year built: 2006

Builder: Hull - Song Cam, Haiphong; completed - Damen, Gorinchem

Engine: 2 x 16-cyl Caterpillar; 5710bhp

Propulsion: 2 x Z-peller units

Bollard pull: 68 tonnes

Gross tonnage: 207

IMO: 9366859

Former name(s):

Later name(s): 07-SVITZER WARDEN

Location: Felixstowe Dock   Date: 18 May 2007

Comments: Built for Adsteam. Here being repainted into Svitzer colours.

Photographer: Derek Sands

Tug: SVITZER SHOTLEY   Year built: 2006   Former name(s): ADSTEAM SHOTLEY-07
Builder: Hull - Song Cam, Haiphong; completed - Damen, Gorinchem   Later name(s):
Engine: 2 x 16-cyl Caterpillar; 5710bhp   Location: Felixstowe   Date: 6 May 2009
Propulsion: 2 x Z-peller units   Comments:
Bollard pull: 68 tonnes   Gross tonnage: 243
IMO: 9366873   Photographer: Ashley Hunn

Tug: SVITZER STANLOW

Builder: ASL, Singapore

Engine: 2 x 8-cyl Caterpillar; 7178bhp

Propulsion: 2 x Voith Schneider units

Bollard pull: 70 tonnes

IMO: 9352793

Year built: 2006

Gross tonnage: 656

Former name(s):

Later name(s):

Location: Mersey estuary   Date: 24 September 2016

Comments: Designed for tanker handling in River Mersey.

Photographer: Richard Clammer

Tug: SVITZER VALIANT

Year built: 2007

Builder: Hull - Song Cam, Haiphong; completed - Damen, Gorinchem

Engine: 2 x 16-cyl Caterpillar; 5710bhp

Propulsion: 2 x Z-peller units

Bollard pull: 70 tonnes

Gross tonnage: 250

IMO: 9366902

Former name(s):

Later name(s):

Location: off Immingham

Date: 16 February 2008

Comments:

Photographer: Simon Smith

Tug: SVITZER SKY   Year built: 2008
Builder: Hull - Song Cam, Haiphong; completed - Damen, Gorinchem
Engine: 2 x 16-cyl Caterpillar; 5710bhp
Propulsion: 2 x directional propellers
Bollard pull: 70 tonnes   Gross tonnage: 250

Former name(s):
Later name(s):
Location: off Portishead   Date: 16 June 2009
Comments:

74   IMO: 9460708   Photographer: Bernard McCall

Tug: SVITZER NARI

Builder: East Isle, Georgetown, Canada

Engine: 2 x 16-cyl Caterpillar; 5438bhp

Propulsion: 2 x Z-peller units

Bollard pull: 60 tonnes

IMO: 9547867

Year built: 2010

Gross tonnage: 381

Former name(s): STEVNS BATTLER-11

Later name(s): 17-STEVNS BATTLER

Location: River Mersey   Date: 23 June 2012

Comments: Chartered by Svitzer from Nordane Shipping, Svendborg, in October 2011; returned from charter in January 2017.

Photographer: Bernard McCall

Tug: SVITZER GELLISWICK

Builder: Qingdao, Qianjin

Engine: 2 x 8-cyl Niigata; 5998bhp

Propulsion: 2 x Z-peller units

Bollard pull: 89 tonnes

IMO: 9412373

Year built: 2008

Gross tonnage: 490

Former name(s):

Later name(s):

Location: Milford Haven   Date: 30 September 2009

Comments: Svitzer ordered 9 tugs from 2 different shipyards to handle the large gas tankers that would use two new terminals at Milford Haven.

Photographer: Steve Kerrison

Tug: SVITZER MUSSELWICK

Builder: Qingdao, Qianjin

Engine: 2 x 8-cyl Niigata; 5998bhp

Propulsion: 2 x Z-peller units

Bollard pull: 89 tonnes

IMO: 9412385

Year built: 2008

Gross tonnage: 490

Former name(s):

Later name(s):

Location: Milford Haven   Date: 14 July 2009

Comments: Three identical sister vessels were built in China.

Photographer: Steve Kerrison

Tug: SVITZER WATWICK

Builder: Qingdao, Qianjin

Engine: 2 x 8-cyl Niigata; 5998bhp

Propulsion: 2 x Z-peller units

Bollard pull: 89 tonnes

IMO: 9412397

Year built: 2008

Gross tonnage: 490

Former name(s):

Later name(s):

Location: Milford Haven   Date: 7 September 2010

Comments: Tugs with red-topped funnels were intended to be dedicated to handling tankers at the South Hook LNG gas import terminal.

Photographer: Steve Kerrison

All three "Wick" tugs assist the ***Al Ghuwairiya*** towards the South Hook terminal at Milford Haven on 19 April 2010. The tug nearest the camera, SVITZER WATWICK, is attached to the tanker in conventional manner as there are no Dutch bollards; the crews of the SVITZER MUSSELWICK amidships and SVITZER GELLISWICK on the port quarter, however, do have suitable bollards on which to attach their lines.

(Steve Kerrison)

Tug: SVITZER LINDSWAY

Builder: Freire, Vigo

Engine: 2 x 16-cyl GE; 7824bhp

Propulsion: 2 x Z-peller units

Bollard pull: 90 tonnes

IMO: 9440758

Year built: 2008

Gross tonnage: 686

Former name(s):

Later name(s):

Location: Milford Haven   Date: 15 May 2010

Comments:

Photographer: Steve Kerrison

Tug: SVITZER WATERSTON
Builder: Freire, Vigo
Engine: 2 x 16-cyl GE; 7824bhp
Propulsion: 2 x Z-peller units
Bollard pull: 90 tonnes
IMO: 9440746

Year built: 2008

Gross tonnage: 690

Former name(s):
Later name(s):
Location: Milford Haven
Comments:

Photographer: Steve Kerrison

Date: 25 October 2009

Tug: SVITZER RAMSEY

Builder: Freire, Vigo

Engine: 2 x 8-cyl Niigata; 5998bhp

Propulsion: 2 x Z-peller units

Bollard pull: 80 tonnes

IMO: 9440899

Year built: 2009

Gross tonnage: 690

Former name(s):

Later name(s):

Location: Milford Haven

Comments:

Photographer: Steve Kerrison

Date: 31 March 2013

Tug: SVITZER CALDEY

Builder: Freire, Vigo

Engine: 2 x 8-cyl Niigata; 5998bhp

Propulsion: 2 x Z-peller units

Bollard pull: 80 tonnes

IMO: 9440887

Year built: 2009

Gross tonnage: 690

Former name(s):

Later name(s):

Location: Milford Haven

Comments:

Date: 19 May 2009

Photographer: Dominic McCall

Tug: SVITZER HAVEN

Builder: Freire, Vigo

Engine: 2 x 16-cyl GE; 7824bhp

Propulsion: 2 x Z-peller units

Bollard pull: 90 tonnes

IMO: 9440760

Year built: 2009

Gross tonnage: 690

Former name(s):

Later name(s):

Location: Milford Haven   Date: 14 July 2009

Comments: Assisting LNG tanker METHANE LYDON VOLNEY towards the Dragon LNG terminal, the first tanker to call at this terminal.

Photographer: Dominic McCall

Tug: SVITZER KILROOM

Builder: Freire, Vigo

Engine: 2 x 16-cyl GE; 8298bhp

Propulsion: 2 x Z-peller units

Bollard pull: 105 tonnes

IMO: 9440904

Year built: 2008

Gross tonnage: 819

Former name(s):

Later name(s):

Location: Milford Haven

Comments: Testing fire monitors

Date: 7 April 2009

Photographer: Steve Kerrison

RESCUE

Tug: SVITZER PEMBROKE
Builder: Zamakona, Pasajes
Engine: 2 x 16-cyl GE; 8298bhp
Propulsion: 2 x directional propellers
Bollard pull: 105 tonnes
IMO: 9557927

Year built: 2010

Gross tonnage: 734

Former name(s):
Later name(s): 14-BOA ODIN
Location: Milford Haven   Date: 1 August 2014
Comments: Built for deepsea towage in addition to harbour work. Sold to
Norwegian owners in 2014 and trading in North Sea and Baltic Sea.
Photographer: Steve Kerrison

Tug: SVITZER TYNE

Builder: Sanmar, Tuzla, Turkey

Engine: 2 x 12-cyl Caterpillar; 4800bhp

Propulsion: 2 x Z-peller units

Bollard pull: 60 tonnes

IMO: 9714111

Year built: 2014

Gross tonnage: 290

Former name(s):

Later name(s):

Location: River Tyne

Comments:

Photographer: Bernard McCall

Date: 23 January 2016

Tug: SVITZER BARGATE   Year built: 2014

Builder: Hull - Ha Long, Vietnam; completed Damen, Gorinchem

Engine: 2 x 16-cyl Caterpillar; 5600bhp

Propulsion: 2 x directional propellers

Bollard pull: 67 tonnes   Gross tonnage: 231

IMO: 9701970

Former name(s):

Later name(s):

Location: Southampton   Date: 21 April 2015

Comments: Appropriately photographed assisting a container ship operated by the parent company.

Photographer: Phil Kempsey

Scouting & Recollecti

The 3rd Parkstone Scout

Chris Harris

First published in 2019

British Library Cataloguing in Publication Data

A catalogue record for this book is available from the British Library.

ISBN 978 1 85794 549 2

Silver Link Publishing Ltd
The Trundle
Ringstead Road
Great Addington
Kettering
Northants NN14 4BW

Tel/Fax: 01536 330588
email: sales@nostalgiacollection.com
Website: www.nostalgiacollection.com

Printed and bound in the Czech Republic

Front cover: **BUDE** The 1968 summer camp for 3rd Parkstone Scouts was held at Bude, and was led by Scouter Ray Cornick (back row, left). It is recorded that the camp ran very smoothly, not least because of the excellent weather, which enabled the planned programme to be closely followed. Clearly a good time was had by all. *Peter Bottomley Collection.*

Above: **LEICESTER** Helping the wider community was always a key objective for 3rd Parkstone. This certificate was awarded to the Cubs when their sponsorship enabled a young athlete from Bristol to take part in the Special Olympic Games held at Leicester in 1989.

Rear cover: **BRYANSTON** The older 3rd Parkstone Cubs also enjoyed opportunities to experience camping. This happy group was photographed at the 1991 summer Cub camp which was held at Bryanston, near Blandford Forum, Dorset. *3rd Parkstone Archive Collection.*

Above: **ASHLEY ROAD METHODIST CHURCH** Throughout its lifetime from 1931 until 2006 the 3rd Parkstone Scout Group was attached to Ashley Road Methodist Church in Upper Parkstone, Poole. Photographed in January 2019, the Methodists no longer hold services in this building, but it is used for worship by the Gateway Church. A reminder of 3rd Parkstone remains, and continues to be much appreciated by pedestrians who wish to pause a while as they walk to the Ashley Road shops – the seats donated by the Scouts in the 1980s (see also page 31). *Chris Harris.*

Foreword

Introduction

When the 3rd Parkstone Scout Group closed there was not only a feeling of a loss of opportunities for the future but also a pervading feeling of a failure to recognise the efforts of all those who had gone before. When a former sixer of the Tawny Six, my friend and colleague from our many years in the bus and coach industry in times gone by, Chris Harris, felt that there was a book to be written I agreed that this would be a fitting tribute. The result is an excellent account drawing on the wealth of records and photographs at our disposal.

So walk again through the doors of Wesley Hall and the Den as the first steps to camps, expeditions, shows, experiences and friendships which have lasted a lifetime.
It is interesting to reflect that summers were not always hotter and filled with sunshine – or perhaps it only rained when the Scouts went to camp!

Ian Gray
Poole, Dorset.

Title Page: **WESLEY HALL** Beavers, Cubs, Scouts, Venture Scouts and adult leaders pose for a 3rd Parkstone group photograph at Wesley Hall in 1991. *3rd Parkstone Archive Collection.*

In August 1907 Robert Baden-Powell held a camp for 20 boys on Brownsea Island in Poole Harbour, Dorset, England; from this small beginning grew the world-wide Scout movement.
Robert Baden-Powell (1857-1941) was a soldier who had become a national hero after his successful defence of Mafeking throughout a 217-day siege during the Boer War. At Mafeking Baden-Powell had been much impressed by the resourcefulness and bravery of the boys that became corps of messengers, and he felt that the Scouting skills of service, observation and woodcraft would be most useful for boys in England. In due course this led to Baden-Powell organising the camp on Brownsea Island, which proved that his training methods were well received by the youngsters, and the event – which included boys from all social classes and from various parts of the country as well as three local lads from Skinner Street Congregational Church in Poole – was a great success.

During 1908 *Scouting for Boys* was published in fortnightly instalments at 4d (just under 2p) a copy. Scout troops were soon being formed around the country, and by 1910 it was estimated that around 100,000 boys aged between 11 and 18 were involved in Scouting. This success led to calls for provision for younger boys who were eager to join the Scouts; accordingly the Wolf Cub section was started in 1916 – this catered for boys aged between 8 and 11 and used Rudyard Kipling's Jungle Book to provide an appealing framework for activities and training. Rover Scouts, for young men over 18, started in 1918.

A number of Scout troops had started in Poole from 1908 onwards. Of particular interest in the context of this book was the 4th Poole Troop. This was formed in 1917 and was associated with High Street Methodist Church; it was led by Mr W. T. Thompson, who was Manager of the Royal Naval Cordite Factory that had been established at nearby Holton Heath in 1915. In order to extend the benefits of

Scouting to boys in Upper Parkstone, a branch of the 4th Poole Troop was inaugurated at Ashley Road Methodist Church. This became a separate troop in its own right – 3rd Parkstone – in 1931. The leaders of the new 3rd Parkstone Troop were brothers Arthur Cockram and Jack Cockram, who had been Scouts with 4th Poole. The photographs and captions in this book illustrate the eventful history of 3rd Parkstone from its inception through to closure following the final Cub meeting in July 2006.

The story is a fascinating one and starts with the almost pioneering days of building up the group in the 1930s. The Second World War followed, with leaders and senior Scouts being called up into the services, while on the 'home front' a number of the Scouts performed useful war work as messengers. Meetings continued, sometimes under very difficult circumstances, but the older Scouts in particular did a sterling job in organising activities. An especially commendable achievement was the publication of a monthly newsletter to keep in touch with those members in the forces or engaged elsewhere on war work.

The post-war period saw 3rd Parkstone go from strength to strength, with 1957 seeing celebrations to mark 50 years of the Scout movement, while in 1966 the Cubs celebrated the movement's 50th birthday. During all of this period from the group's inception in 1931, 3rd Parkstone had been meeting at Wesley Hall in Parkstone; this dated from 1923 and had been intended as a temporary structure when it was built, but by the mid 1960s there were finally plans to replace it with a new purpose-built church hall and youth centre. The new premises were officially opened on Saturday 24 June 1967, and were very much appreciated by the Cubs, Scouts and other organisations associated with Ashley Road Methodist Church.

In many ways the following 30 years perhaps marked the zenith of 3rd Parkstone. The Cub and Scout sections provided a wide variety of experiences and adventures for local youngsters, and as the photographs and captions in this book illustrate, the programme offered kept well up to date with the changing times. In 1991 3rd Parkstone marked its 60th birthday with the release of a professionally produced film *Old Gold and Royal Blue* which celebrated the first 60 years of the group, including interviews with people who could remember the early days.

In 1991 3rd Parkstone had more than 100 boys spread across four sections – Beavers, Cubs, Scouts and Venture Scouts. But just over a decade later, as the 21st century gathered pace the group found itself facing serious leadership problems. Reluctant resignations owing to work pressures together with retirements came at a time when suitable replacements could not be found. The 3rd Parkstone Scout Troop was merged with that of St Aldhelm's Church, Branksome, in 2004, while the Beaver Colony was transferred to St Peter's Church (1st Parkstone) in 2005. The Cub Pack continued for a little longer, but the final Cub meeting was on 26 July 2006, bringing down the curtain on 75 years of valuable work done by 3rd Parkstone.

It is sad to report that Ashley Road Methodist Church has also subsequently closed, while the 1967 hall has been demolished and housing now occupies its former site in Wesley Road. But the great work done by 3rd Parkstone lives on in the memories of these who were lucky enough to have been associated with that group over the years; the experiences gained have helped, and continue to help, many people achieve success in their adult lives.

I feel very honoured to have been asked to write this book, as I was only very briefly associated with 3rd Parkstone during the 1960s. It has only been possible to produce this illustrated history thanks to the wonderful record books and photograph albums that were maintained by the group throughout the 75 years of its existence, so I say a very big 'thank

you' to everyone who has been involved with this over the years. Thank you also to everyone who has contributed material or encouraged this project, including Ray Cornick, Peter Bottomley and Janet Cockram, plus Brian Jackson for scanning the photographs and providing technical advice. And in particular, a special 'thank you' to Ian Gray, the final Group Scout Leader at 3rd Parkstone, who invited me to write this book and without whose help over many months it could not have been completed.

I hope you will enjoy reading 3rd Parkstone Recollections, and that it will bring back happy memories for you if you have ever been a beaver, Cub, Scout, Venture Scout or adult leader/supporter.

Chris Harris
Poole, Dorset.

POOLE The success of the first Scout camp on Brownsea Island in Poole Harbour during August 1907, followed by the publication of *Scouting for Boys* the following year, quickly led to Scout troops being formed across the country; it was estimated that around 100,000 young people were taking part in Scouting by 1910. This progress continued during the following decade. It was in 1917 that Mr W. T. Thompson, Manager of the then recently established Royal Naval Cordite Factory at Holton Heath, formed the 4th Poole Scout Troop which was attached to High Street Methodist Church in the town centre; among the members of the 4th Poole Troop were brothers Arthur and Jack Cockram. Leaders, Scouts and Cubs from 4th Poole were photographed during the 1920s. *Janet Cockram Collection.*

Above: **SCOTLAND** The 4th Poole Scouts were quite adventurous in their choice of locations for camp. On one occasion they travelled north to Scotland, where this photograph, showing Mr Thompson with some of the Scouts, was taken. The Minister at Ashley Road Methodist Church felt that Scouting should also be available for boys in Upper Parkstone, and a branch of the 4th Poole Troop ran at that location for a number of years until it became a separate Troop in its own right in 1931, with Arthur and Jack Cockram as leaders. A camp in Scotland was an achievement that was to be repeated many years later by 3rd Parkstone, whose 1973 summer camp took place near Pitlochry (see page 27). *3rd Parkstone Archive Collection.*

Right: **15 JUNE 1931** saw the Proclamation of 3rd Parkstone. The Proclamation, as recorded in the log book and reproduced here, reads: 'This day must be written down as a Red Letter Day in the long history of the 4th Poole and 3rd Parkstone troop of Boy Scouts. It was until this ever to be remembered date that the two Troops were one under the name of 4th Poole. It was then that we of the Branksome Section come forward and go out into the world full of true Scout Spirit to help to spread the great Brotherhood of Scouts. AU REVOIR 4TH POOLE – ALL THE BEST.' Also recorded on the same page of the log book is the Registration of 3rd Parkstone (number 13167) – this reads: 'It was on October 1st that we were duly registered at Head Quarters and the Troop Officers were: SM: A G Cockram, CM & ASM: W J Cockram. A Rover Crew was started, but no Rover leader was obtainable owing to the age limit but the Rover mates are carrying on quite well. Then came the selection of Group colour which was finally decided as Blue and Gold.' *3rd Parkstone Archive Collection.*

Left: **LYTCHETT MATRAVERS** The 3rd Parkstone troop went from strength to strength. In November 1933 Jim Young was the first member to gain his 1st Class badge, while two members of the Troop were awarded King's Scout badges in 1934. A weekend camp at Lytchett Matravers in the summer of 1934 was enjoyed by 25 members, as seen here. In November 1934 Arthur Cockram became Group Scout Master, a position he would hold for 40 years until 1974. *3rd Parkstone Archive Collection.*

Below: **WESLEY ROAD** The headquarters of the 3rd Parkstone troop was at Wesley Hall, in Parkstone. The 3rd Parkstone Scouts and Cubs were photographed at Wesley Hall in 1931, shortly after separating from 4th Poole. *3rd Parkstone archive collection.*

Above: **WESLEY ROAD** The Dorset County Rally and Banner Guard Competition for 1935 was held at Preston, near Weymouth, from 7-11 June. Although 3rd Parkstone came six points behind the overall winners, they did come first in their district, winning the banner from the holders, 7th Parkstone, by one point. The winning team is seen here at Parkstone; the building in the background was a former bakery that was used by the Scouts in addition to Wesley Hall; it was known as The Den. *3rd Parkstone archive collection.*

Below: **LANGTON MATRAVERS** 3rd Parkstone Scouts' summer camp for 1935 was held near Langton Matravers in Dorset. It took place from 3-10 August and was attended by around 20 boys. A parade to Langton Matravers Methodist Church on the morning of Sunday 4 August was followed by swimming at Dancing Ledge. There was an initiation ceremony for those attending Scout camp for the first time, and useful badge work was carried out. It was noted that four Scouts passed their 'cook' badge; it also mentions that one of them attempted to make some toffee, but as it did not turn out quite right he called it fudge instead. *3rd Parkstone archive collection.*

Above: **LANGTON MATRAVERS** The log of the camp notes that shopping for provisions was done in Swanage – wonder if this rather magnificent hand cart was used? As well as visiting the town for shopping, the lads enjoyed spending an afternoon and evening at the Swanage Regatta. It was noted that the week went all too quickly, and it was time to return home on Saturday 10 August. *3rd Parkstone archive collection.*

Below left: **LANGTON MATRAVERS** was a popular spot for camping during the early years of the 3rd Parkstone troop. The summer camp for 1938 took place between 30 July and 6 August, and by all accounts the weather was somewhat mixed. As usual, the camp ran from Saturday to Saturday; it was noted that during the Wednesday night there was a 'grand thunderstorm' with vivid lightening which the following morning was found to have brought down a tree across the nearby road. It was reported to have rained for much of the rest of the camp, but nonetheless everyone enjoyed themselves – including the lads photographed here – and it seemed all too soon when the lorry arrived to take them home on Saturday 6 August. *3rd Parkstone archive collection.*

Below right: **LYME REGIS** The 1939 summer camp at Lyme Regis was noted as being 'one of the wettest to date' but hastens to add that everyone thoroughly enjoyed it. By the Thursday the kitchen area had been reduced to a swamp, and it was felt to be much too wet to attempt a camp fire that evening, so the lads went to the cinema in Lyme Regis instead. There were a few intervals of slightly better weather, during one of which a hike across the Devon border to Uplyme was enjoyed, while fine weather eventually blessed the camp on the Friday afternoon, allowing various Scout games to take place. *3rd Parkstone archive collection.*

WESLEY ROAD Circumstances immediately after the outbreak of the Second World War in September 1939 precluded the troop meeting in Wesley Hall for the time being, so the Scouts decided to clear out The Den and hold the meetings there. A former bakehouse, The Den had a range at one end; this was removed, the wall chipped back and a fireplace installed. The other walls were match-boarded and distempered. As can be seen, they did a fine job.

The dark days of the Second World War took their toll on 3rd Parkstone. During the early months of 1940 a combination of the blackout and an exceptionally severe winter reduced attendance at meetings, but the troop carried on and helped the war effort by arranging waste paper collections and undertaking messenger work with the ARP services. On Friday 10 May 1940

the Germans invaded Holland, Belgium and Luxemburg; this led to the British government cancelling the forthcoming Whitsun bank holiday on 13 May, but 3rd Parkstone decided to continue with their planned camp at Langton Matravers during Whit week, the lads setting off from The Den on their bicycles at 2.30pm on the Saturday. By all accounts this was a wonderful week away from the grim realities of war, as beautifully illustrated by this excellent drawing that has been scanned from the log book. *3rd Parkstone archive collection.*

SANDBANKS FERRY A weekend camp at Langton Matravers in early June 1940 was attended by around 20 boys and was blessed by what was described as 'splendid weather'. The lads cycled to the camp site, using the Sandbanks Ferry across the mouth of Poole Harbour to Shell Bay. Subsequently Sandbanks Ferry was suspended in July 1940, and the service was not resumed until July 1946 – so the lads made this trip just in time. Two of the party are seen on the ferry, with part of the Haven Hotel just visible in the background. The shadow of war fell faintly on the camp; it was noted that the tents had to be camouflaged so that they would be less visible from the air. Nonetheless it is clear that a good time was had by all, and the account of the camp concludes by saying 'There's no place like Langton'. *3rd Parkstone archive collection.*

PARKSTONE Although the group had been able to resume using Wesley Hall for meetings, these again had to be transferred to The Den for a while in November 1940 when the Hall was used as a refuge for several local people who had sadly been made homeless by bombing; it became available for troop meetings again from 6 December. Group Scout Master Arthur Cockram – Skip – joined the Royal Army Medical Corps at Newquay on 12 December 1940; the 3rd Parkstone log book records that 'four of our keenest Scouts, including the GSM and two ASMs are in HM Forces. Two more are in the Home Guard. The CM is working at a government training centre in Southampton, and four more Scouts have been evacuated from the district.' Skip is seen in his RAMC uniform. *3rd Parkstone archive collection.*

Above left: **KINGSTON** A party at Wesley Hall on 4 January 1941 for Scouts and friends was attended by fewer friends than anticipated owing to air-raids; as there was a good complement of Scouts there it was recorded that no food was wasted. A further air-raid alert sounded just after tea, but it was reported that the party continued without interruption. Four days later, the founder of the Scout movement, Lord Baden-Powell, died; a district parade to a memorial service at St Peter's Church, Parkstone, took place on Sunday 19 January. The summer of 1941 saw a number of enjoyable hikes into the Purbeck area. On 21 June the Scouts cycled to Corfe Castle, then walked to Kingston and Chapman's Pool – where they were unable to go right down to the coast owing to defence regulations. The steep climb back to Kingston on a June day was rewarded by a welcome drink of cool water from the pump outside Kingston Post Office. *3rd Parkstone archive collection.*

Above: **BADBURY RINGS** An autumn cycle ride to explore part of East Dorset included Wimborne, Hinton Parva and Witchampton and culminated in a wide game at Badbury Rings; some of the group are seen setting out from there for the homebound journey. By mid-1941 a monthly bulletin was produced and sent to all 3rd Parkstone members in the forces; this was very much appreciated by recipients. *3rd Parkstone archive collection.*

CRANBROOK ROAD Roy Courage had been promoted to Patrol Leader of the Peewit Patrol in 1939. Following the outbreak of the Second World War he also did much useful work as an ARP messenger (as seen here) and was attached to the First Aid Post in Cranbrook Road, Parkstone. He subsequently left Parkstone, moving to Newport (Monmouthshire); he wrote to the 3rd Parkstone Troop in 1942 saying that he had joined the 7th Newport Scout Troop, which was attached to the local YMCA, and that he was patrol leader of the Eagle Patrol. In March 1942 a separate Senior Patrol was formed at 3rd Parkstone which was able to do useful local war work. *3rd Parkstone Archive Collection.*

SHERBORNE For the first time since the outbreak of war, the Dorset County Scout Banner Guard Competition was held over the weekend of 26-27 August 1944. The event was held in the grounds of Sherborne Preparatory School and 19 teams entered. The competition included campcraft, leadership, smartness and general Scout work, with various tests undertaken. The winning team was the Woodpigeon Patrol of 3rd Parkstone, who are seen with the Banner in the photograph (standing L-R) P. Geddes, A. Macdonald, M. Fendley and D. Humphrey (seated) C. Thresher and L. Fisher. A celebration social event was held at Wesley Hall on Thursday 14 September 1944; among the guests attending was the Mayor of Poole, Alderman Joseph Bright. *3rd Parkstone Archive Collection.*

WESLEY ROAD Saturday 30 September 1944 was also a red-letter day for the 3rd Parkstone Troop. This was the occasion of the District Athletic Sports Competition, which the 3rd Parkstone Team won quite decisively, being 13 points ahead of their nearest rivals, 15th Southampton. This excellent result was the reward for nearly two months of regular training sessions at the Branksome Recreation Ground in Alder Road. The winning team were photographed near Wesley Hall; a note explains that the cup was not available when the photograph was taken, being still with the engravers. *3rd Parkstone Archive Collection.*

LANGTON MATRAVERS Everyone rejoiced when VE Day marked the end of the War in Europe in May 1945. On Saturday 4 August that year members of the 3rd Parkstone Scout Troop departed for their first week-long camp after the war. The weather was rather mixed and included a thunderstorm on the Wednesday evening. Nonetheless everyone enjoyed activities that included hikes, swimming at Dancing Ledge and wide games. The happy campers are seen on one of the sunny days. *3rd Parkstone Archive Collection.*

CHARISWORTH Scouts from 3rd Parkstone attended a District Camp at Charisworth, near Blandford, that was held over the Whitsun weekend, 10-12 June 1946. This event was attended by a number of troops, including 1st Oakdale, 5th Poole and 3rd Dorchester. Apparently the weather forecast had predicted 'fine and rather warm' conditions, but in the event heavy rain on the Sunday evening leaked through a new bell tent to such a degree that those attempting to sleep in it eventually had to take refuge in the main marquee. Fortunately the three day camp did also see some fine weather; during one of these more clement interludes the opportunity was taken to have a kit inspection. It was also noted that as the group returned to Parkstone by lorry during the early evening of Whit Monday, 12 June, the sun was shining from a cloudless sky! *3rd Parkstone Archive Collection.*

LANGTON MATRAVERS For the week-long summer camp in 1946, 3rd Parkstone Scouts returned to one of their favourite locations – Langton Matravers. This was held from Saturday 3 August until Saturday 10 August, and the weather was very mixed but everyone attending had a great time. Sunday 4 August was one of the fine days, and two 'unexpected visitors' turned up at the camp site – to the delight of two of the patrol leaders, who the log book notes were 'unavailable for the remainder of the day'. *3rd Parkstone Archive Collection.*

Left: **BRANKSOME** It was in March 1950 that what was then the Borough of Poole Boy Scouts Association launched an appeal for a suitable memorial for Lord Baden-Powell. This appeal was answered very generously in 1951 by Lord Ventry, who gave part of his land at Lindsay Hall, Lindsay Road, Branksome, for this purpose. Following a further five years of fund-raising and hard work, Olave, Lady Baden-Powell, opened the BP Memorial Training Ground and Hall on 9 June 1956, as photographed here; Arthur Cockram, Group Scout Master of 3rd Parkstone, is seen in the centre at the rear. The BP Memorial Training Ground was used by Scouts until the late 1980s, when the land was sold following the death of Lord Ventry. *3rd Parkstone Archive Collection.*

Below: **CHALBURY** The 3rd Parkstone Scouts summer camp for 1956 was held at Chalbury in Dorset. On 13 August the Cub pack was taken by bus to Chalbury for a day out at the Scout camp, where they enjoyed various games and sports with the Scouts; some of the Cubs are seen during a break for lunch. *3rd Parkstone Archive Collection.*

WESLEY ROAD, PARKSTONE In many ways the year 1957 was one of celebration for Scouts in Poole. On Saturday 6 April the various troops in the area took part in a show commemorating 50 Years of Scouting, which took place at 7.30pm in the Great Hall at Parkstone Grammar School (at that time located at Ashley Cross). The presentation illustrated the history of the movement, the section allocated to 3rd Parkstone being *The Advent of Cubbing, 1916*. Then on the next day a Scout Thanksgiving Service was held at St Aldhelm's Church, Branksome, to commemorate the centenary of the birth of the late Lord Baden-Powell in 1857; hymns included *Praise, my Soul, the King of Heaven* and *Onward, Christian Soldiers*. Celebrations continued on the following Friday, when 3rd Parkstone Cubs and Scouts staged a concert at Wesley Hall which included a play *Skull and Crossbones* by the Cubs as well as musical items. Cubs and Scouts of 3rd Parkstone, together with their leaders, were photographed on the stage at Wesley Hall on Friday 12 April 1957. *3rd Parkstone Archive Collection.*

WOOKEY HOLE On 28 August 1957 3rd Parkstone Cubs enjoyed a coach outing to Wookey Hole in Somerset. It is recorded that the boys 'greatly enjoyed going into the caves, and a stop was made for tea and games on the journey home'. The party was photographed beside the coach at Wookey Hole; Akela John Willis is seen second from the right at the rear of the group. *3rd Parkstone Archive Collection.*

ASHLEY ROAD, PARKSTONE The Scouts and Cubs regularly held Church Parades, forming up in Kipling Road and marching along Ashley Road to the Methodist Church. After the service they would march back along Ashley Road to Highland Road, where they would be dismissed. After morning service on a rather damp Sunday in April 1959 the boys are marching back along Ashley Road towards Highland Road on Parade to mark St George's Day. *3rd Parkstone Archive Collection.*

GILWELL PARK Occupying a site of more than 100 acres in Epping Forest, not far from Chingford, Gilwell Park is well known as an activity centre for Scouts and Guides, having been used as such since 1919. On 18 May 1959 (Whit Monday) parents arranged an outing to Gilwell for 3rd Parkstone; it was a wonderful day, enjoyed by all, and after a picnic lunch they were given a conducted tour around the Gilwell grounds. *3rd Parkstone Archive Collection.*

Left: **GILWELL** A number of training courses for leaders take place at Gilwell Park. The most important is the Wood Badge, an award originated in 1919 and one of the highest accolades for a Scout or Cub leader. Janet Cockram, seen front right in this photograph taken at Gilwell on 18 May 1959, gained her Wood Badge, and in 1960 took over from John Willis as Cub leader (Akela). *3rd Parkstone Archive Collection.*

Right: **CRANBROOK ROAD, PARKSTONE** On the evening of Friday 19 July 1962 the older Cubs in the 3rd Parkstone pack departed by lorry from Wesley Hall for a weekend camp at Verwood. Along the way, the lorry called at the Cockram household to pick up food supplies for the camp. The boys are clearly in great spirits as the lorry proceeds along Cranbrook Road. The weather was excellent throughout; everyone had a fantastic time and it seemed all too soon when the lorry returned to the camp site at 7.30pm on Sunday 21 July to bring the campers home. *3rd Parkstone Archive Collection.*

CRANBROOK ROAD, PARKSTONE For three years running, 1962, 1963 and 1964, Cubs from 3rd Parkstone won the totem competition. Teams from up to 15 Cub packs in the area took part in this competition, which involved the participating Cubs in a series of tests. Sixers and Seconds from 3rd Parkstone also attended the annual county rally at Dorchester; that is where this group of lads, with John Bottomley (Bagheera) and Janet Cockram (Akela) were making for when photographed in Cranbrook Road, prior to making their way to the station to catch a train to Dorchester. The author, then Second of the Tawny six (he was later promoted to Sixer), can be seen front left wearing a light-coloured raincoat and leaning rather insouciantly against Skip's garden wall. Notice that Cranbrook Road still had gas street lamps in the early 1960s. *3rd Parkstone Archive Collection.*

NOMANSLAND The warm summer evening of Wednesday 23 June 1965 was the occasion of a coach outing to Nomansland for 3rd Parkstone Cubs and their parents. Everyone brought along a picnic tea, which was supplemented by slices of a delicious cake made by Mrs Cockram. A game of rounders was played by the Cubs and most of the parents. Before boarding for the homeward journey, some of the Cubs are seen beside one of the two coaches that provided the transport for this occasion; it is recorded that the hire of these 41-seat vehicles cost £7 for each coach. *3rd Parkstone Archive Collection.*

VERWOOD July 1965 saw 15 of the more senior Cubs and their leaders attend a weekend camp at Verwood. This was favoured by glorious weather and featured wide games, a walk around the Verwood area and a camp fire. There was a Parade to Verwood Methodist Church on the Sunday morning. On the morning of Saturday 17 July 1965 (left to right) Paul Dyke, Neil Blaney, Barry Dyke and Andrew White are seen reading the camp notices; that camp notice board lasted for many years, being used at Cub camps and Scout camps. *3rd Parkstone Archive Collection.*

CRANBROOK ROAD, PARKSTONE The totem competition for 1965 took place on 23 October. Photographed at Skip's house before taking part, the 3rd Parkstone team consisted of Clive Jay, Richard Selby, Paul Dunford, Neil Blaney, Andrew White and Robert Read. Whilst they did not do quite as well as the 3rd Parkstone teams of the previous three years, they nonetheless came in second with a very creditable 555 points. *3rd Parkstone Archive Collection.*

BRANKSOME RECREATION GROUND Early in 1966 fifteen local packs took part in the annual six-a-side football competition for Poole Cubs which was held at Branksome Recreation Ground. This event was won by 3rd Parkstone, who beat 1st Lilliput in the final to win the cup. The winning team consisted of Colin Legg, Stephen Corbin, Robin Tuttiett, Andrew White, Paul Stacey and Timothy Tuttiett. To reach the final, 3rd Parkstone had beaten 3rd Poole, 4th Parkstone and 1st Broadstone in the preliminary rounds. *3rd Parkstone Archive Collection.*

WESLEY ROAD, PARKSTONE The Cub movement was 50 years old in 1966. A number of events were put on, both locally and nationally, to celebrate this milestone. Cubs from 3rd Parkstone attended a Cub Jubilee Day at Gilwell Park on 2 July, and at the end of the year the pack received a certificate from Sir Charles Maclean in recognition that the boys had completed all parts of the Chief Scout's Challenge for the year. This photograph of the 3rd Parkstone pack, together with their leaders, was taken inside Wesley Hall in 1966. *3rd Parkstone Archive Collection.*

LANGTON MATRAVERS The summer of 1966 saw the publication of the Advance Party Report following the deliberations of a committee that had been set up in 1964 by the Chief Scout, Sir Charles Maclean, to review the Scout and Cub movement and to plan for the future. The Report heralded many changes, including to uniforms and even to the Scout Law and Promise. Also, the terms Wolf Cubs and Boy Scouts were to be completely dropped, with members being referred to as simply Cubs or Scouts. When these members of the 3rd Parkstone pack were photographed proudly holding up their flag at Langton Matravers in the late summer of 1966, their days of being officially known as Wolf Cubs were numbered. *3rd Parkstone Archive Collection.*

VERWOOD The weekend camp for the older Cubs in July 1967 was once again blessed by good weather; here the boys were photographed when they were eager to tuck in to their dinner! *3rd Parkstone Archive Collection.*

Ashley Road Methodist Church

PARKSTONE - POOLE

Souvenir Programme

of the

OPENING CEREMONY

and

DEDICATION

of the

New Church Hall & Youth Centre

Saturday, June 24th 1967

Two Shillings

WESLEY ROAD, PARKSTONE From its beginnings in 1931, the 3rd Parkstone Troop had met at Wesley Hall in Wesley Road. This building had been put up by Ashley Road Methodist Church in 1923 for youth work and other social activities. The 1923 hall was only ever intended to be a temporary structure, but in fact it lasted for 44 years before it was replaced on the same site by a new church hall and youth centre. This was officially opened on Saturday 24 June 1967; a short service in the church at 4.15pm was led by Rev Herbert Simpson, General Secretary of the Department for Methodist Chapel Affairs and a previous Minister at Ashley Road. The service opened with the hymn *Ye Servants of God, Your Master Proclaim* and the address was given by Rev Simpson.

The service was followed at 5pm by prayers of dedication in the new hall that were led by Rev R. C. Stonham, Chairman of the Southampton District of the Methodist Church. Built by Burt & Vick Ltd., at the time of opening a total of £16,451 was available towards the cost of the new premises, and every effort was being made to complete the project free of debt although some further funding would be required to achieve this. The facilities at Ashley Road Methodist Church were certainly very well used in 1967; the church was able to offer meetings on every night of the week, with activities suitable for all ages providing something for every member of the family. The Cubs were photographed after their first pack meeting in the new hall. *3rd Parkstone Archive Collection.*

WESLEY ROAD, PARKSTONE For clarity, we will continue to refer to the 1967 structure as Wesley Hall; it occupied the same location as the previous 1923 building, and many people continued to speak of it as Wesley Hall. The Cubs were quick to take advantage of their modernised surroundings and presented an adventurous entertainment for parents and friends. Entitled The One and Only Parkstone Cub Scout Circus, this was written by Group Committee member Mr Godfrey, with music provided by Mrs Quincey at the piano. *3rd Parkstone Archive Collection.*

VERWOOD In 1968 Ian Gray, who had been a Cub in a pack latterly based at St Osmund's Church, Parkstone, decided to join the 3rd Parkstone troop when the time came for him to go up to Scouts. This was to prove a very significant event in the history of 3rd Parkstone, as in the fulness of time Ian would become the Group Scout Leader. Here Ian is seen (front row, second from left) after joining 3rd Parkstone, at a Scout camp in Verwood, where he and his friends have constructed a fence with quite an elaborate revolving gate. *Peter Bottomley Collection.*

DELPH WOODS On Saturday 15 May 1971 a team from 3rd Parkstone consisting of M. Anderson, K. Graham, I. Stranks, R. Barksfield, J. Redwood and S. Woodward took part in the Poole District Cub Scout Competition. The programme included pitching tents, collecting wood, lighting a fire, cooking and washing up. This was followed by potted sports and a wide game and the day ended with a camp fire. Photographed during the cooking element of the competition, the log book does not record the position achieved by the 3rd Parkstone team! *3rd Parkstone Archive Collection.*

WESLEY ROAD, PARKSTONE The 1971 Christmas Fayre for Ashley Road Methodist Church, held in Wesley Hall, included a stall of Christmas goods that had been made by 3rd Parkstone Cubs and Scouts. Group Chairman Mrs J. Wright is seen on the left with Skip (Group Scout Leader Arthur Cockram). Akela (Janet Cockram) is on the right. Some of the Cubs subsequently went carol singing at Stanfield Road Elderly Persons' Dwellings. *3rd Parkstone Archive Collection.*

BROWNSEA ISLAND Brownsea Island in Poole Harbour, the birthplace of the Scouting movement, had passed into the ownership of the National Trust in 1962, and the following year was opened to visitors. From the late 1960s onward Cubs and Scouts from 3rd Parkstone have made regular visits to Brownsea; some Cubs are seen enjoying this visit, which was noted as working towards their 'Conservation' badge. Notice the peacock – Brownsea Island now has a large population of these beautiful but noisy birds, which are native to South Asia; it is likely that they were imported during the Edwardian era, a period when they were introduced at a number of British stately homes. *3rd Parkstone Archive Collection.*

BUDE Camp was always one of the highlights of the year for the Scouts. Hikes, wide games and outings were blended with songs round the camp fire, the fun of open-air cooking and, of course, sleeping under canvas. A feature of all 3rd Parkstone Scout camps was a water fight, hugely enjoyed by all as seen in this photograph taken near Bude in the summer of 1968. *Peter Bottomley Collection.*

BOURNEMOUTH For the 3rd Parkstone Scout summer camp in 1973, Scout Leader Peter Bottomley wanted to do something a little more adventurous than the usual week under canvas somewhere in the West Country. A two-week camp near Pitlochry was decided on, taking place from Saturday 18 August until Saturday 1 September. The boys attending the camp travelled by train from Branksome station, but as Peter pointed out 'There is a fair bit of gear to be taken to a Scout camp, apart from all the personal kit, so for us to get it to Scotland needed a separate method of transporting it there.' Peter therefore drove the kit to and from the camp site in 3rd Parkstone's first minibus, PEL 350G; this vehicle had started life as a 15cwt van, but following acquisition by the Scouts bench seats had been fitted down the sides and windows put in. Back in those days there were fewer motorways and Peter started his journey north well before the Scouts, setting off after completing a morning at work on Thursday 16 August 1973. As can be seen, some of Peter's colleagues had 'decorated' the vehicle in readiness for the long journey. *Peter Bottomley Collection.*

LOCH TUMMEL This vista is known as the Queen's View, so called because Queen Victoria was especially fond of it. The site of the 1973 camp was nearby, and all of the tents had a view of Loch Tummel when the flaps were open. Activities included raft building on the Loch, hiking, games and visits to local towns. Camp was struck on Thursday 30 August; the final two nights were spent in a Scout hall in Edinburgh so as to attend the Military Tattoo on Friday 31 August. This proved a very fitting climax to what everybody agreed had been the most rewarding Scout camp in the history of 3rd Parkstone to date. The Scouts returned to Branksome by train on the Saturday morning, while Peter brought the equipment back in PEL 350G — quite an intrepid journey that he made via Gilwell and London, finally arriving back in Parkstone around 3pm on Sunday 2 September, having travelled exactly 2,000 miles in PEL 350G since it was loaded prior to departure for the camp. *Peter Bottomley Collection.*

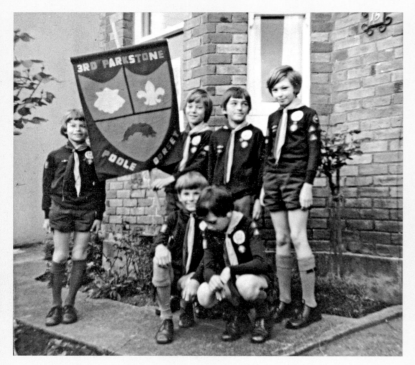

Left: **CRANBROOK ROAD, PARKSTONE** A happy group of Cubs with the 3rd Parkstone banner outside Skip's house in the late 1970s. Unfortunate that the young gentleman crouching down on the front right of the photograph seems more interested in his friend's shoe than in smiling for the camera! *3rd Parkstone Archive Collection.*

Right: **BALSTON ROAD, PARKSTONE** An interesting and successful fund-raising venture for the International Year of the Child in the late 1970s was sponsored by a brand of washing-up liquid. The Cubs visited people offering to do their washing up for them in exchange for a donation – all of which went to help children in Nepal; the only reward for the Cub was the satisfaction of a job well done and a knowledge that they were making a real difference for children in another part of the world. The Cubs took everything required to do the washing up (except water and the kitchen sink) with them in a special pack supplied by the manufacturers of Sunlight Lemon Liquid, and the job cards given to the Cubs included a seven-step guide for washing up. Three of the Cubs are seen with Mollie Fendley ready to set out on their mission of washing up for the people of Parkstone. *3rd Parkstone Archive Collection.*

WESLEY ROAD, PARKSTONE In 1977 we celebrated the Silver Jubilee of Her Majesty Queen Elizabeth II. A day out for the 3rd Parkstone Cubs that year was a trip to London that included seeing the Changing of the Guard at Buckingham Palace at 1100 followed by visits to the Tower of London and HMS *Belfast* during the afternoon. The highlight of the day was in the late afternoon when the Cubs visited the Royal Chelsea Hospital and presented a Silver Jubilee blanket that they had designed and knitted for the pensioners. The Cubs are seen with the blanket prior to departing from Wesley Hall in Parkstone. *3rd Parkstone Archive Collection.*

LYMINGTON PIER STATION The 1978 summer camp took place on the Isle of Wight; public transport was used to travel to the site. Having alighted from the 4 CIG unit forming the Brockenhurst to Lymington branch train, the lads walk down the platform to join the ferry *Cenwulf* for the thirty minute crossing to Yarmouth. Ian Gray, now in a leadership role, is seen second right in the photograph. *3rd Parkstone Archive Collection.*

Left: **EASTLEIGH** During the late 1970s and early 1980s the BBC broadcast a television programme called *Hey Look, That's Me* which aimed to inspire youngsters to take up various hobbies or interests. On 21 October 1979 3rd Parkstone Scouts took part in a Go Kart Rally at Eastleigh that was arranged by this programme. Transport from Parkstone to this event was provided by Hants & Dorset in the form of 70-seat rear-entrance Bristol FL6G double-deck bus 7687 LJ. New in December 1962, 7687 LJ was quite a rare vehicle – it was one of only 45 Bristol FLs to be built out of a total production of 5,218 Lodekkas of various types for Tilling Group bus operators in the UK. Hants & Dorset had 12 of the 45 FLs; by the time this photograph was taken at Eastleigh 7687 LJ had been repainted into National Bus Company poppy red livery; it was withdrawn from service in 1980. *3rd Parkstone Archive Collection.*

Right: **SOUTH HAVEN POINT** A great achievement during 1980 was walking, in stages, the scenic and dramatic Dorset Coast Path. The path runs for 86 miles from Lyme Regis to this point (the southern terminal of the Sandbanks ferry) including some very steep ascents and descents, but rewarded by beautiful and spectacular views. Scouts and parents are seen having completed the final section of the walk; Ian Gray is standing on the left of the photograph, while Tony Kellaway, then Headmaster of South Road School in Poole, is third from the right at the rear. Across the mouth of Poole Harbour behind Ian Gray notice the Haven Hotel visible in the background; during the early years of the 20th century Marconi carried out some of his experiments in radio here. *3rd Parkstone Archive Collection.*

WESLEY ROAD, PARKSTONE The year 1981 marked the Golden Jubilee of the 3rd Parkstone Scout Troop. This photograph was taken in January 1981 in Wesley Hall, showing the Venture Scouts, Scouts and Cubs, together with their leaders and others who had been involved during the previous 50 years. In particular, Arthur Cockram ('Skip' from 1931 until 1974) is standing fourth from the left on the middle row, while Ray Cornick ('Scouter' from 1957 until 1970) stands second to the right of Arthur. Seated in the centre of the group of Cubs and Scouts (left to right) are Janet Cockram (Akela), Adrian Lankester (Group Scout Leader) and Ian Gray (Scout Leader). The gentleman standing to the left at the rear is David Stranks, who later was to run the Scout Shop for a number of years. *3rd Parkstone Archive Collection.*

ASHLEY ROAD, PARKSTONE
Throughout their history, 3rd Parkstone Cubs and Scouts held regular church parades to Ashley Road Methodist Church (see also page 17). Here we see the special Jubilee Parade in the spring of 1981 approaching the church. As part of their Jubilee celebrations the Cubs and Scouts provided a public bench seat outside the Church; the £150 cost of this was raised in various ways, including sales of the group photograph seen on this page. A second seat was also later provided by the Scouts' fund-raising efforts. Although sadly the building is no longer in use as a Methodist Church and the 3rd Parkstone Scout Troop has disbanded, the seats donated by the Scouts are still in place at the time of writing (2019). *3rd Parkstone Archive Collection.*

Right: **HAMWORTHY** On 23 February 1983 3rd Parkstone Scouts were the guests of the Royal Marines at Hamworthy. Transport for the visit was provided by a special relief Hants & Dorset bus that ran from Uppleby Road to Rockley Sands, the Scouts all paying the appropriate transfer fare that then existed between those points. The highlight of this visit was the landing craft base, where the lads had chance to experience transport that was somewhat more exciting than a bus; this group are really enjoying their sea trip in a rigid raider. *3rd Parkstone Archive Collection.*

Below: **WESLEY ROAD, PARKSTONE** A presentation evening was held on 15 June 1984 when 3rd Parkstone Scouts were awarded with two prestigious trophies. John Sier, Area Youth Officer, is seen presenting the district table tennis league trophy. Also presented on this occasion was the Portman Building Society Trophy for Community Involvement; this competition was open to Scout groups within the Borough of Poole, who had to submit projects illustrating the involvement of members in giving service to the community. *3rd Parkstone Archive Collection.*

Above: **WESLEY ROAD, PARKSTONE** A great achievement in the summer of 1994 was the provision of 20-seat Bedford coach PYU 11F for the use of 3rd Parkstone Cubs and Scouts. This followed three years of fund-raising; a grant from the Area Youth Committee and money from the Poole lottery also helped toward the purchase of this vehicle. It was painted in the appropriate gold and blue colours for 3rd Parkstone by Bill Dixon, coach painter for the Wilts & Dorset Bus Company. The coach was officially launched by Mrs Heather Cornick, seen standing in the doorway; group chairman Ray Cornick (wearing the striped tie) stands just to the rear of the doorway. Arthur Cockram stands on the left of the photograph. *3rd Parkstone Archive Collection.*

Above right: **PEAK DISTRICT** The Scout summer camp for 1984 was ten days based at Elton, near Matlock Bath. The camp had an activity theme based on 'three Cs' – Caving, Canoeing and Climbing. Peter Cornick, son of Ray and Heather Cornick, clearly very much enjoyed caving. *3rd Parkstone Archive Collection.*

Right: **KINDER Scout** At 2,087 feet above sea level, Kinder Scout is the highest point in the Peak District and a truly spectacular place to visit. On 24 April 1932 this was the scene of a mass trespass by around 500 walkers, an act of civil disobedience that had the happy result of helping to secure much better access rights to open countryside for everyone to enjoy. While camping in the Peak District in the summer of 1984 3rd Parkstone Scouts took advantage of the freedom won for them over 50 years earlier by walking to Kinder Scout, with much valued guidance provided by local Scout Jim. *3rd Parkstone Archive Collection.*

BADEN-POWELL HOUSE, LONDON The autumn half term of 1986 saw 25 members of 3rd Parkstone Cubs enjoy a pack holiday at Gilwell Park. During the outward journey on Monday 20 October the coach stopped at Baden-Powell House in London for everyone to have lunch before visiting the nearby Natural History Museum. Baden-Powell House is a Scouting hostel and conference centre; it was opened in 1961. The granite statue of Baden-Powell is by Don Potter. The weather during the week was generally wet, but everyone had a great time. Even the journey home on Friday 24 October was something of an adventure, with Parkstone eventually being reached around 10.00pm rather than the scheduled time of 5.30pm. *3rd Parkstone Archive Collection.*

GILWELL PARK Fortunately the weather was much kinder when 3rd Parkstone took part in the Gilwell Cub Day on 20 June 1987. Activities on offer included canoes, swimming, pillow fight poles, a blindfold trail through a 'hot steamy jungle', monkey bridges and much more. Organisations who had provided displays and exhibitions included the London Fire Brigade, the British Transport Police, the Metropolitan Police and British Telecom – whose display featured what was described as the world's largest telephone. To end the day there was a grand camp fire at 4.45pm. As can be seen, the 3rd Parkstone boys entered gleefully into the spirit of the event – all concerned requiring a shower before boarding the coach home. *3rd Parkstone Archive Collection.*

WATERCRESS LINE A 3rd Parkstone Cub Pack holiday in October 1987 featured a visit to the Watercress Line heritage railway at Alresford, including a ride to and from Alton and a visit to the locomotive sheds at Ropley. Here the Cubs are standing beside Southern Railway Class 'U' No 31806. This locomotive was originally built at the Southern Railway's Brighton Works in 1926 as one of the ill-fated Class 'K' locomotives, named *River Torridge*. It was rebuilt as a Class 'U' locomotive, also at Brighton Works, in 1928. Withdrawn from British Railways service in January 1964, over 23 years later the preserved locomotive was admired by the Cubs who enjoyed this experience of a form of transport that would have been commonplace when their fathers had been of an age to attend Cubs (steam trains were eliminated in the Parkstone area in July 1967). *3rd Parkstone Archive Collection.*

POOLE FIRE STATION On 10 May 1989 3rd Parkstone Cubs visited Poole Fire Station. Not long after they arrived, a teleprinter message came through from Dorset Fire Brigade Control at 7.04pm: 'Welcome to Poole Fire Station – have a good evening. All the best from Brigade Control'. The Cubs certainly did have a good time; they all had a ride in a fire engine, and were also encouraged to climb up on the vehicle. But we suspect that what the lads enjoyed the most was the opportunity to squirt their leaders with a hose! *3rd Parkstone Archive Collection.*

POOLE PARK The 3rd Parkstone Scout Group was 60 years old in 1991. One of a number of events to mark this significant milestone was the planting of a tree in Poole Park on 21 April 1991. All of the boys in the 3rd Parkstone Group attended the ceremony; the youngsters wearing grey uniforms at the front of the group are Beavers. The 3rd Parkstone Beaver Colony had commenced in 1989, providing fun and activities for boys aged between 6 and 8 before they moved up to Cubs. *3rd Parkstone Archive Collection.*

Above: **POOLE CIVIC CENTRE** Another event held to mark 60 years of 3rd Parkstone was a Group Reunion held on 5 October 1991 at Poole Civic Centre. In the back row we see (left to right) John Main (who had been the Mayor's Scout in 1975/6 to Denis Gooding), Gordon Carter, Mike Hampton, Ian Wright, (name unknown), (name unknown), Brian Brown and Graham Brown, while the front row comprises (left to right): Tim Smith, Peter Bottomley, Alex Wright, Jay Fendley, Janet Cockram, Stuart Fendley, 'Q' Corke, Ray Cornick and David Corke. *3rd Parkstone Archive Collection.*

Right: **POOLE CIVIC CENTRE** The major project to mark 60 years of 3rd Parkstone was the production of a film, *Old Gold and Royal Blue,* which illustrated the history of the Group to date. This was produced by Stephen Nimmo, Simon Clunie-Curtis, Peter Munday and Nick Taylor, who are seen in this photograph. *Old Gold and Royal Blue* proved to be a wonderful living record of 3rd Parkstone, including commentary from people who had been in the Group right from the start. In 1991 3rd Parkstone had more than 100 boys spread across four sections – Beavers, Cubs, Scouts and Venture Scouts. *3rd Parkstone Archive Collection.*

Above left: **FERNY CROFTS** Situated in the heart of the New Forest and about a mile from Beaulieu Road station, Ferny Crofts is an excellent 31-acre Scout Activity Centre. The site was purchased by Hampshire Scout Council in November 1975, and has been used for Scout camps and other activities from 1976 onwards with the facilities and amenities available having been increased over the years. 3rd Parkstone continued the celebrations of their 60th anniversary with a group weekend at Ferny Crofts in the autumn of 1991. Whilst there everyone enjoyed a slice of this very special cake. *3rd Parkstone Archive Collection.*

Above: **WESLEY ROAD, PARKSTONE** The signs fitted to the roof rack ensured that everyone knew who was being conveyed in the 3rd Parkstone Scout Group minibus during the mid-1990s. By this time all of the minibus drivers were required to undergo a training course; Scout Leader Ian Gray is seen being presented with his certificate. *3rd Parkstone Archive Collection.*

Left: **FERNY CROFTS** The group was delighted to welcome Gwen Cockram (widow of Arthur) and Nellie Cockram (widow of Jack) to the Ferny Crofts event. These ladies indeed provided a link right back to when Arthur and Jack Cockram had started the 3rd Parkstone Scout Group in 1931, and over the years both Gwen (left) and Nellie had contributed a great deal to the success of the group – including showing great kindness, helpfulness and encouragement to Cubs and Scouts who visited their homes to carry out various tasks in connection with badge work. The group weekend was much enjoyed by everyone and was a very fitting culmination of the events organised for 3rd Parkstone's 60th anniversary year. *3rd Parkstone Archive Collection.*

ST JOHN'S CHURCH HALL, PARKSTONE
Unusually, the 1995 3rd Parkstone Christmas Fayre was held in St John's Church Hall in Ashley Road, Parkstone. A highlight was the installation of Denis Gooding as Life President. Denis had been a 3rd Parkstone Scout as a boy; much later, when he was Mayor of Poole in 1975/6 he donated half the monies raised by the Mayor's Charity that year for the development of a Scout hall on land donated by Lord Ventry at Branksome (see page 15). In the event it turned out that this money was eventually used in 1986 to purchase what had been The Parkstone Young Men's Sporting Club in Layton Road; these premises were formally re-opened by Denis Gooding in October 1986 as the headquarters of Poole Scout Council and the Poole Scout Fellowship (see also pages 41 and 43). At the 1995 Christmas Fayre, Group Scout Leader Ian Gray looks on as Denis gives an enthusiastic speech having been made Life President. *3rd Parkstone Archive Collection.*

NOTHE FORT, WEYMOUTH Located at the entrance to Weymouth Harbour, Nothe Fort was built over a 12-year period between 1860 and 1872. It ceased to have a defence role in 1956 and was purchased by the local authority in 1961. Now one of the best-preserved forts of its type, it is open to the public and includes a number of fascinating displays and exhibits. As we can see from the photograph, 3rd Parkstone Cubs certainly enjoyed their visit to Nothe Fort on 10 June 2000. *3rd Parkstone Archive Collection.*

AVON COUNTRY PARK Cub summer camp in 2000 took place from 29 July until 1 August at Avon Country Park. A very enjoyable few days in the open air, it also provided the opportunity for the Cubs to develop their badge work. Here we see Cubs Peter, David and Joel working towards their Map Reader badge; the requirements for this included being able to understand and use the key of an Ordnance Survey map, being able to use six-figure grid references, understanding contour lines and using an Ordnance Survey map as part of an outdoor activity. The boys are clearly working with great interest. *3rd Parkstone Archive Collection.*

WESLEY ROAD, PARKSTONE A memorable occasion for the Cubs in 2000 was the evening when Group Life President Denis Gooding came to their meeting. They are listening attentively as he outlines amusing anecdotes of the time when he was a member at 3rd Parkstone many years previously. Denis spent much of his life serving his community. He was a stoker in the Royal Navy during the Second World War, and in the post-war period worked in the ambulance service, and then in 1974 worked on the night staff at Poole Hospital. He represented Newtown ward as a Labour member of Poole Council for many years, and was Mayor of Poole in 1975-6. Denis died in December 2008 at the age of 86; his lasting memorial is The Denis Gooding Centre in Layton Road, Parkstone (see also pages 39 and 43). *3rd Parkstone Archive Collection.*

WESLEY ROAD, PARKSTONE Venture Scouts, for young people aged between 16 and 20, were introduced following the Chief Scout's Advance Party Report in 1967, and were the first element of the Scout movement to be opened up to female membership (in 1976). A Venture Unit at 3rd Parkstone had commenced in 1983. Venture Scouts enjoyed an active programme including outdoor activities and community service. They wore the same uniform as leaders, but could choose between a tie or a neckerchief. Members of the 3rd Parkstone Venture Unit were photographed in 2000; second from the left on the back row is Ragen Bartaby, who at the time of writing is the District Commissioner for Scouts in the Poole area. *3rd Parkstone Archive Collection.*

TEFFONT EVIAS During the autumn half term in October 2000 3rd Parkstone Cubs visited Farmer Giles Farmstead at Teffont Evias in Wiltshire. Bottle-feeding some of the animals was popular, and here we see the group on a traditional-style tractor – note the very appropriate wellington boots worn by everyone. *3rd Parkstone Archive Collection.*

Left: **LIGHTHOUSE, POOLE** The year 2000 saw Janet Cockram complete 40 years as Akela of the 3rd Parkstone Cub Pack. This outstanding service was recognised by the Borough of Poole in the form of a Poole Achievement Award, which was presented at the Lighthouse (Poole Arts Centre). Janet was photographed after receiving her award, with Group Scout Leader Ian Gray (left) and District Commissioner Geoff Dennis (right). *3rd Parkstone Archive Collection.*

Right: **WESLEY ROAD, PARKSTONE** Cub meetings traditionally began with the 'Grand Howl' –'Akela, we will do our best!'. The pack photo album entry for the Cub meeting on Wednesday 22 November 2000 is headed 'Akela, we will do our best to keep it a secret'. In this endeavour they were successful, and therefore Janet was surprised and delighted to be greeted with a very special cake, iced in the 3rd Parkstone colours of old gold and royal blue, together with cards and gifts from the Cubs. *3rd Parkston Archive Collection.*

Left: **DENIS GOODING CENTRE, LAYTON ROAD, PARKSTONE** A

party to mark Janet's 40 years as Akela was held at the Denis Gooding Centre on Saturday 25 November 2000. Very properly, this included another cake, and Janet was assisted in cutting this by Ian

Wright – who had been one of her first Cubs back in 1960. The Denis Gooding Centre has its origins in a club for young men established by Buckland Road Baptist Church in 1919. Purpose-built club premises in Layton Road were opened in 1936, but sadly the building was destroyed during an air raid in 1941. After much fund-raising the present building was completed in 1951, and it was acquired by Poole Scout Council in 1986 (see also pages 39 and 41). *3rd Parkstone Archive Collection.*

Above: **WESLEY ROAD, PARKSTONE** A Cub pack consists of a number of groups of six boys, which (quite logically) are known as sixes. At Cub meetings the sixes work and play together as teams; the sixes are called by various colours. Thus, in January 2001 the 3rd Parkstone pack consisted of five sixes – Browns, Yellows, Blacks, Reds and Greys. At that time the Black six, seen in the photograph, in fact consisted of seven boys. Each of the sixes had their own area of the hall, which was denoted by attractive screens as seen here. The boys themselves were encouraged to make their six area look as bright and 'Cubby' as possible. *3rd Parkstone Archive Collection.*

Above right: **ST CLEMENT'S ROAD, NEWTOWN** Trauma teddies were pioneered by the Australian Red Cross in the 1990s. The teddies helped distract young children and keep them occupied when something traumatic was going on around them. During the evening of Thursday 22 February 2001 the Founder's Day Service for Cubs in the Poole East District took place at St Clement's Church, Newtown, and at the conclusion of the service a donation of £250 was given to Dorset Fire and Rescue Service to go towards the purchase of trauma teddies for the Fire and Rescue Service to give to young children who are distressed in emergency situations such as fires or collisions. *3rd Parkstone Archive Collection.*

Left: **KINGSTON LACY**
Ancestral home of the Banks family from the 17th century onwards, Kingston Lacy house, park and gardens were bequeathed to the National Trust following the death of Henry John Ralph Banks in 1982, and were opened to the public in 1986. 3rd Parkstone Cubs visited Kingston Lacy on 17 May 2003, taking with them a number of bird boxes that they had made. Under the direction of the National Trust personnel they also helped with outer outdoor conservation tasks in the park, including the removal of the plastic covers from the trunks of recently planted saplings. *3rd Parkstone Archive Collection.*

Left: **BOURNEMOUTH AVIATION MUSEUM** A project undertaken by the Cubs in the spring of 2003 was the construction of model aeroplanes to help the boys gain their 'Air Activities' proficiency badge. This was followed up by a visit to the fascinating Bournemouth Aviation Museum at Hurn. Here some of the Cubs are about to have a look over Handley Page Dart Herald 401 aircraft G-BEYF; with seats for 50 passengers, this had been new in 1963, and had passed to Channel Express in 1988; it was withdrawn from service in April 1999. *3rd Parkstone Archive Collection.*

BROWNSEA ISLAND On 20 September 2003 3rd Parkstone Cubs and their leaders enjoyed a visit to Brownsea Island in Poole Harbour; the birthplace of the Scout Movement. Brownsea Island has been owned by the National Trust since 1963, and the inscribed stone seen in the photograph was set up in 1967. Carved by Don Potter, the inscription reads: 'This stone commemorates the experimental camp of 20 boys held on this site from 1st-9th August 1907 by Robert Baden-Powell later Lord Baden-Powell of Gilwell Founder of the Scout and Guide Movements.' *3rd Parkstone Archive Collection.*

Above: **WESLEY ROAD, PARKSTONE** On Wednesday 26 November 2003 Janet Cockram, having reached the age of 65, retired from her position as Akela of 3rd Parkstone Cubs. Janet had taken on the role of Akela in 1960, and a number of her former Cubs – grown men by 2003 – came to the Cub meeting to thank Janet and to wish her well. The evening included a slide show illustrating highlights of the past 43 years, and it proved to be one Cub meeting where Janet was able to relax and put her feet up! Janet's place as Akela was taken by Christine Gilbert (previously Baloo), who said of Janet 'She has been great fun, very patient and kind. It will seem very funny without her.' *3rd Parkstone Archive Collection.*

Above centre: **WESLEY ROAD, PARKSTONE** At the Cub meeting on 26 November 2003 Geoff Dennis, District Commissioner of Poole East District Scouts, presented Janet with an engraved plaque, a bouquet of flowers, a hand-made card and many other gifts. Janet was able to look back at the photo-album memories of her time as Akela with justified satisfaction. *3rd Parkstone Archive Collection.*

Above right: **BROWNSEA ISLAND** Unfortunately by 2004 the 3rd Parkstone Scout Group was facing serious leadership problems. Scout Leader Ron Southcott had to resign owing to work pressures; no replacement could be found, so the Scout Troop merged with that at St Aldhelm's Church, Branksome. Also in 2004 Christine Gilbert relinquished her position as Akela, requiring emergency arrangements to be put in place. In 2005 the Beaver colony and some boys and leaders from the Cub pack were transferred to 1st Parkstone (St Peter's Church). For those Cubs unwilling or unable to transfer a small Cub pack was retained; Janet came out of retirement to act as leader, ably assisted by Laurence and Claire Mizen plus various parents. The final 3rd Parkstone Cub meeting was on 26 July 2006; Group Scout Leader Ian Gray wrote at the time "It had always been my intention to hand over the Group in a stronger position than when I took it over. I did not want to be the last Group Scout Leader and it will be forever a regret that the closure came to pass on my watch. I hope those that follow will not judge those of us who were responsible too harshly."

It is very fitting that a reminder of the great work that 3rd Parkstone carried out with several generations of local boys remains in the beautiful St Mary's Church on Brownsea Island; the hassock on the right was made to commemorate 50 years of 3rd Parkstone, 1931-1981 – how appropriate that it is now at the birthplace of Scouting. *Janet Cockram Collection.*

Index